J 282353
FOR-T

The Politics of
Italian Foreign Policy

THE
POLITICS
OF
ITALIAN
FOREIGN
POLICY

NORMAN KOGAN

FREDERICK A. PRAEGER

Publisher · New York

BOOKS THAT MATTER

Published in the United States of America in 1963 by
Frederick A. Praeger, Inc., Publisher
64 University Place, New York 3, N.Y.

Library of Congress Catalog Card Number: 63–9434

Printed in the United States of America

To the memory of
my father and brother

PREFACE

There has been a growing awareness in recent years among students of international politics, both professional and amateur, of the role the domestic social and political environment plays in influencing, perhaps determining, foreign policy. Studies of an earlier day centered on the international environment—the international political system, international institutions, and reciprocal interstate influences. Traditional diplomatic histories seemed rather two-dimensional, concentrating on the exchanges between diplomats and the reports from emissaries stationed abroad, while neglecting the attitudes, aspirations, political forces, and movements at work within the country's boundaries.

My intention is not to deride and criticize this earlier approach, which produced many outstanding works, but rather to explain the assumptions underlying the material to be presented here. The recent emphasis on the internal environment is not intended to disparage earlier viewpoints or to claim that the study of the international environment is not essential to an understanding of a nation's foreign policy, but I wish to redress the balance to some degree. The growth of modern mass societies, with the impact of mass needs and demands, even though they may remain unarticulated through the political process; the presence or absence of identifications or the rejection of traditional identifications—all these affect the making of political decisions, including foreign-policy decisions. This holds true even in a society that may be very oligarchic and permits only a limited number of individuals or groups to exert influence upon decision-makers.

I have operated under the assumption that a society's attitudes about the nature and goals of man, about the reasons for participation in politics, and about the expectations of the results of such participation, affect not only the motives of political decision-makers but their methods of operation as well. I have assumed that there is more than one way of discovering these attitudes. They may be revealed by sociological, literary, or opinion studies. They may be deduced from a society's history, especially its political and diplomatic history. They may be illuminated by direct examination.

I have used all these approaches to ascertain how political decisions affecting foreign policy are made in Italy, the kinds of decisions made, and the forces operating to influence them. Rather than making a case study of a particular decision, tracing all of its ramifications, I have attempted a broad investigation of the Italian political system as a whole, orienting the investigation toward questions of foreign policy.

The opportunity for direct examination was made available to me through the generosity of a number of individuals and organizations who furnished time, funds, introductions, and information. I was able to spend the academic year 1957/58 in Italy by virtue of a sabbatical leave granted by the University of Connecticut. Additional funds came from the Committee on Comparative Politics of the Social Science Research Council. Colleagues and friends in the United States and Italy gave me the benefit of their wisdom and provided invaluable introductions. Through them, I was able to interview Italian politicians, administrators, academicians, and journalists. These were all invariably kind, helpful, and courteous, and they do not personally deserve, nor are they in any way responsible for, some of the harsh strictures and judgments in the following pages. I owe a great debt of gratitude to my wife, whose help in putting the manuscript into shape was indispensable. However, I must take sole responsibility for any errors of fact, judgment, or interpretation.

NORMAN KOGAN

February, 1963
Storrs, Connecticut

CONTENTS

TABLES

I

Backgrounds of
Political Behavior

1

SOCIAL AND POLITICAL ATTITUDES

The essential characteristics of a political system cannot be divorced from the social environment; attitudes toward politics and politicians flow from attitudes toward life. The attitudes and behavior patterns of a small and homogeneous group can be discovered more easily than those of a larger and more heterogeneous group, and generalizing about the latter is risky. Studies of national attitudes or character, both sociological and literary in nature, face the perils associated with all attempts to generalize on an inadequate base, whether the inadequacy results from the restricted nature of the sample analyzed or from the subjectiveness of the investigator's "feeling" for a culture and people.

Despite these limitations, certain recent works using either sociological or literary techniques have produced results that in general reinforce each other. The characteristic attitudes that will be described have direct relevance to the kinds of politics that will be played because politicians are a product of society and are unlikely to differ radically from it. There will be modifications in this relationship if the politicians tend to be drawn from a restricted social group; then, obviously, the attitudes of this group will be of prime importance. It must be proved, however, that a restricted group is relatively immune to prevailing attitudes in the larger society before the evidence taken from the larger society can be rejected as worthless.

Italy is fundamentally a peasant society; about 30 per cent of the population today is directly working the land. It is also a society of villages and towns, populated by families removed at the most a generation or two from a rural environment and retaining many peasant attitudes. The southern peasantry is especially important, because its internal migrations have left an impact on both the rural and urban nonsouthern regions. It has filled the ranks of the state bureaucracy through its notably ambitious sons or grandsons, and this bureaucracy is spread all over Italy.

Edwin C. Banfield, in an intensive sociological investigation of a southern Italian peasant village, summed up the basic hypothesis of peasant living in the phrase "amoral familism," which he defined as the pursuit of one overwhelming goal: "Maximize the material short-run advantage of the nuclear family; assume that all others will do likewise." [1] He observed further: "The world being what it is, all those who stand outside the small circle of the family are at least potential competitors and therefore also potential enemies. Toward those who are not of the family the reasonable attitude is suspicion." [2]

Banfield found one central theme other than material gain in the peasant's existence: "cutting a good figure" [3] (*fare una bella figura*). The desire to make an impression, obtain notice, respect, admiration, and some glory underlies human behavior in every country, but the necessity to cut a good figure and to avoid cutting a bad one (*brutta figura*)—especially to avoid appearing ridiculous—is particularly acute in Italian society, everywhere, up and down the social scale. This necessity is behind the concern for titles and the hunt for honors, which naturally become more meaningless the more widely they are distributed.

Banfield found little difference between peasant and upper-class attitudes:

Among the gentry self-interest is not universally material advantage in the short run. A few gentlemen would probably be willing to make some sacrifice of material goods to obtain prestige, public recognition, "glory. . . ." In Montegrano [the name is fictitious] there are no opportunities to obtain glory in any manner whatever. At present then, the gentry are as exclusively preoccupied with material advantage as are the peasants, and so it is approximately correct to say that amoral familism is the ethos of the whole society—of the upper class as well as of the lower.

He cites a communication from J. S. McDonald, an Australian demographer, who

. . . comments that in Calabria "homogeneous values are shared by all classes; differences in behavior between classes are more a function of the distribution of social and technological power than of different value systems." [4]

This picture of the social world in the Italian south gets confirmation from literary descriptions by both natives and foreigners. The Sicilian Sebastiano Aglianò, in summing up the characteristics of Sicilian society, points out that they are the characteristics of Italian society in general but heightened to an extreme degree. There is an obsession with authority; respect for hierarchy, dignity, titles, and influence; the avoidance of regular channels of operation; and the utilization of political leverage for even the smallest questions. The people are impressed by power and possessions, and this leads to a servility toward others who may be able to help or hurt them, who may be able to give recommendations or protection.[5]

After spending a number of years teaching in Florence and traveling in central and northern Italy, a French writer, Jean-François Revel, rather unkindly generalized his experiences in terms similar to the above portrait of the south. He described the values of Italian life as security, respectability, appearances. Happiness was a product of wealth. "The Italian people are the only people I know who are really and totally materialistic without distinction of class or of profession." [6] This extreme and unqualified statement may indicate only a limited knowledge of other peoples on the part of the author, but it reflects a given condition even if its comparative aspect remains unacceptable.

A basic underlying condition is the absence of social solidarity, a sense of isolation that leads to a lack of trust in other human beings or in social groups. All the writers referred to earlier note this, and the following quotation from an Italian stonemason epitomizes it: "No one outside my family is really interested in my personal well-being, and this is why I don't belong to any organizations." [7] This lack of solidarity is reflected in the Italians' skeptical view of their compatriots. They do not impute to other Italians any generosity of motives and behavior. No foreigner can calumniate Italians or Italy half so effectively as the Italians themselves. Thus Elena Croce, daughter of Benedetto Croce, writes of the "omnipresent and corrosive dishonesty in economic behavior," of the modern development of a "mass culture which is all the more suffocating because it does not contain in itself . . . any rational or coherent social purposes. . . ." She can describe Italy as "a country composed exclusively of individuals and minorities [not in an ethnic or religious sense], almost totally lacking in any instinctive or constructive social tradition." [8]

The relative absence of private voluntary organizations is an additional indication of the lack of solidarity. This is most marked in the south. In the center and the north, the existence of many cooperatives, unions, and mutual-benefit societies may give a contradictory impression. But in many cases the members have a purely instrumental attitude toward their participation, expecting at best only a concrete material benefit, withholding a sense of identification with the larger group, and often suspecting the motivations of the group's leaders. The leaders sense this, and their mistrust of the loyalty and solidarity of their followers makes them reluctant to delegate authority and responsibility downward. As a result, decision-making in organized groups, both public and private, tends to be highly oligarchical; the few people at the top retain all the levers of command within their own grasp.

Social stratification remains very strong, in the north as well as in the south. In the industrial and commercial north and center, class lines are more subtle and complex than in the peasant south, but they are there. Today, as in the past, talent is recognized, rewarded, and socially accepted once it has been demonstrated and proved. The Church on occasion has made a Pope out of a prelate who began life as a peasant boy. Some Roman emperors were of Balkan-peasant origins; Renaissance *condottieri* and nineteenth- and twentieth-century intellectuals, politicians, and business leaders rose from nowhere. But these few exceptions did not in the past, nor do they now, indicate that class lines are breaking down. Italians are as much concerned with classifying people today as they ever were; categorizing individuals into social strata is still a necessity.* To an ever-increasing extent, the only channel for upward mobility is the formal educational system, still bookish and literary in orientation.[9] The university degree has become the prerequisite to virtually every position of value in private or public life.

Subservience to hierarchy is accompanied by subservience to authority, in both political and nonpolitical fields. Giuseppe Borgese claims that it is the tyranny of the family group in which most Italians are brought up that instills a subsequent conformism and obsequiousness to other kinds of tyranny.[10] Whatever the origins, the phenomenon is striking. It manifests itself in a variety of ways. There is a uniformity of style in clothes; everybody must be dressed like everybody else.[11] In the literary world, Giosuè Carducci exercised a kind of benevolent dictatorship for thirty years before the turn of the century,[12] and Croce for fifty years thereafter.[13] In political life, even during the liberal period prior to World War I, there were the "disguised" dictatorships of Agostino Depretis, Francesco Crispi, and Giovanni Giolotti.[14]

Materialism, appearances, glory, servility and conformism—these social characteristics are far from uniquely Italian. They are found everywhere in varying degrees. Their accentuated character on the Italian scene is a product of mass poverty, centuries of submission to foreign domination, and visible reminders of the ancient, glorious eras when Italy was the political, intellectual, and cultural center of the Western world.

From his analysis of the village life of the southern peasant, Banfield formulated a number of propositions about political attitudes. He stated them in categoric terms for emphasis, but they are derived not merely by deduction from his fundamental concept of amoral familism, but also by interview and examination of actual behavior: (1) Material gain in the short run will be the only motive for concern with public affairs; (2) public affairs are for officials, not for private citizens; (3) whatever group is in power is assumed to be self-serving and corrupt; (4) there is no connection between abstract

---

* Ambassador Pietro Quaroni found it significant enough to note in his memoirs that Ferenc Nagy had the "face of a petty-bourgeois intellectual." Pietro Quaroni, *Valigia diplomatica* (Milan: Garzanti, 1956), p. 277.

principle (i.e., ideology) and everyday behavior; (5) a claim to be inspired by public welfare rather than private advantage is regarded as fraudulent; and (6) officeholders and professional people regard their positions as weapons to be used for private advantage.[15]

Out of this background emerges a general operating assumption that political decisions, whether on policy or personnel, are rarely made on the merits of the issue. It is expected that the public explanation for a decision is never the real one; it is taken for granted that personal power or material interest is really behind every decision. This bias is held not merely by those who are personally remote from politics but ready to suspect the worst; it prevails at all levels of government among those who are directly involved and who actually know the people described in the following anonymous quotations:

"X is a neo-Atlanticist because the Atlanticists* have the post he wants and he has to have a reason for getting them out so he can get in."

"Y advocates a qualitative credit policy because he wants Z's job, and since Z advocates a quantitative credit policy, Y has to counter with a different one to justify replacing Z."

Obviously these explanations fail to explain why the Atlanticists or Z holds the policies he does, but the usual response to this question is that it is in his material interest or the interest of the group he represents to advocate such a policy. A variant of the personal-power explanation is the personal-failure explanation:

"X became a neo-Atlanticist because he was turned down for promotion by the Atlanticists and he wants to overthrow their policy in retaliation."

"W is a *dirigista*† because he could not get to power in private industry and is now anti-*liberista*." Such explanations are oversimplified, but they are suggestive of the atmosphere of political attitudes.

A similar assumption prevails regarding personnel decisions: that these are made not on merit but on the basis of connections and through possession of the right recommendations.‡ "When

---

* See page 136 for an explanation of this term.
† See page 96 for an explanation of this term.
‡ The problem of personnel selection has been expressed by Seymour Martin Lipset as follows: "The wealth level will . . . affect the extent to which given

one is accustomed from an early age to consider intrigue (the 'recommendation') as 'the only means of getting ahead,' in school, in court, in the bank, at city hall, one cannot avoid seeing in both private and public life a game of protection, a clash of influence, more or less efficacious, the prevalence of capricious sympathies and antipathies." [16]

The assumption that participation in politics is warranted only by personal material and prestige gains was dominant at the end of the nineteenth century. Fascism promoted the deterioration of the political system by its encouragement of gross fraud, corruption, cynicism, and political immorality.[17] Recent analyses of voting behavior have shown the heavily materialistic basis of the political choices made by the electorate, contrary to the common saw that Italians vote "out of sentiment and resentment." International Research Associates made an analysis of seventy-six communes in which the Communist vote shifted substantially—up or down—between 1948 and 1953. *Local* economic issues were found to be the overwhelming determinants of voting shifts. General economic doctrines (socialism, capitalism, etc.) were not important, nor were general economic conditions unless they had direct *local* effect. Favors or local improvements did change votes. Clientelism retained some influence, but this was also based on economic attachments. National issues were not factors.[18] In another study involving all provinces, the political geographer George Kish listed the following factors as determining voting behavior (in order of importance): (1) economic status, (2) position in the social order, (3) historical tradition of the family, and (4) effectiveness of the party organization in the locality.[19]

The Italians' emphasis on personal gain undermines whatever bonds of social solidarity and respect for legality were left after Fascism fell. In a nation of lawyers and law-school graduates, there is no sense of legality among either the governors or the governed.

---

countries can develop 'universalistic' norms among its civil service and politicians (selection based on competence; performance without favoritism). The poorer the country, the greater the emphasis which is placed on nepotism, i.e. support of kin and friends." "Some Social Requisites of Democracy: Economic Development and Political Legitimacy," *The American Political Science Review*, March, 1959, p. 84.

Nor is there a sense of the legitimacy of the republic, even among its economic and political beneficiaries.[20] The result is that there is no confidence that the law will protect one's rights or fulfill one's expectations. Rights and expectations require protectors, friends, influence.[21]

Fascism also eroded both social consciousness and class solidarity. The sense of joint endeavor for a good cause flamed again during the resistance movement in World War II and for a short time thereafter. By the middle of the 1950's, that flame appeared to be almost extinguished. Hopes of a better future through state, community, and even trade-union action had, to a great extent, disappeared. Italy appears to be sharing the general postwar European experience of depoliticization. Families appear to be preoccupied exclusively with their own concerns and unable or unwilling to connect their own fate with that of the community at large.[22] Regardless of political orientation, Italian professors past middle age despair of the present generation of university students. Traditionally, the students provided the politically conscious elite and were the first to man the barricades. Today they avoid politics and political commitment. They strike only to get out of examinations or studies. Marxist and Christian trade-union leaders bemoan the *embourgeoisement* of the Italian worker, who has lost his class and union solidarity, and, up to now, has not found a surrogate.

There is a chasm between the people and their political institutions. This is a different thing from the old cry of the opposition parties, which are usually prone to claim that the government in power is really unrepresentative of the country (*pays légal* versus *pays réel*). What is meant here is that substantial portions of the "popular masses" are "outside the state." This is recognized and admitted by representatives of the government in power. Giovanni Gronchi, then President of Italy, in a speech to the Parliament, referred to "those working masses and middle classes whom universal suffrage has conducted to the doorstep of the state's edifice without introducing them effectively to where political direction is exercised." [23] On another occasion, he defined the proper object of governmental activity as "the reconciliation of the people with the state about which we dream and toward which we work."[24]

The present fracture recalls the old distinction between the rulers and the popular masses. Italian writers since the nineteenth century have emphasized the dichotomy between the "political class" (*classe politica*) and the "popular masses" (*masse popolari*). When they talk about public opinion, they mean the opinions of members of the political class, not the popular masses, whose opinions can find expression only on election day. Within the political class, there is a smaller group identified as the "ruling class" (*classe dirigente*).* Perticone includes in the political class those who *exercise* political rights and influence and can exert economic pressure. He defines the ruling class as that small collection of individuals who hold the power of government as leaders of political parties (in power and in opposition) and economic circles.[25] Doxa, an Italian opinion-polling agency, defined members of the political class in personal terms as those who own things, are effectively literate, and have responsibility and make decisions. They belong to the following groups:

1. Ministers, undersecretaries of state, senators, deputies
2. High functionaries of the state, including university professors (who are state employees)
3. Proprietors and directors of large undertakings—industries, firms, financial institutions
4. Members of the professions—lawyers, doctors, writers, journalists, artists, etc.[26]

A slightly different classification is presented below. The political class is composed of writers (journalists, *littérateurs*, professors of subjects such as history, politics, and economics; clerical writers on political subjects), lawyers, doctors, and politicians. The ruling class is composed of the key politicians (the members of the party executive directorates, *direzioni*), the directors-general in the ministries (the highest career posts), Vatican prelates, and big-business leaders. The key politicians are the only members of the ruling class who pay attention both to members of the ruling class and to members of the political class; the other members of the ruling class pay attention only to each other.†

* Doxa reverses the classifications, calling the larger group the ruling class and the smaller one the political class.
† This classification and description of attention orientations was given to me by a director-general in one of the ministries.

Most politicians come from the Italian middle and lower bourgeoisie. The majority have a legal education, although they may not have practiced law. Big-business leaders and titled aristocrats, with some exceptions, do not directly enter politics, although they are in politics behind the scenes. The Marxist parties began to introduce working-class elements into political leadership prior to World War I, but even here the leadership was furnished mainly by middle-class intellectuals.[27] Since World War II, middle-class elements have strengthened their leadership in the proletarian parties and the trade unions. An examination of the central committees of these parties and the executive boards of the unions indicates that they consist chiefly of professors (the title is applied to both secondary and university teachers) and doctors (of law, commerce, or letters, because the degree of doctor is regularly granted upon successful completion of the university program). As new elements moved into positions of influence in Italian society, they came to resemble their predecessors more than they differed from them.[28] Passing from class to class was possible for individuals before, during, and after Fascism, but class lines remained firm.[29] Imitation of the pattern of life of the social groups into which they moved became more rather than less common. Before World War I, socialist leaders led the life of poverty of the masses they represented. Today Communist, Marxist Socialist, and Social Democratic leaders have villas in the country and luxurious apartments in town, and their mentality has adjusted to their surroundings.

Out in the country, away from Rome, the situation is the same. The local lawyers, professors, and accountants run the party sections.[30] A typical Socialist Party organization in the countryside follows this pattern: ". . . the social distinctions between the section leaders and the ordinary members are being accentuated; little by little, the posts of section secretaries and councilors are being taken over by lawyers, pharmacists, merchants, and accountants, while the sharecroppers, farm laborers, and small peasants disappear from the leadership positions." [31] This is not a phenomenon peculiar to the Socialist Party. It exists in all the larger parties that have a mass base, and is absent, if at all, probably only in the very small parties whose sections are composed of middle-class intellectuals.

In other words, the members of the political class greatly resemble each other and are responsive to many of the same motivations, in spite of the wide ideological divergences between the various formal philosophies they represent. Distinctions between right and left, loudly publicized, suddenly seem to disappear when a deal (*combinazione*) is made to share posts, patronage, jobs, honors, and profits. This phenomenon, called transformism, in Italian political life, has a long history.[32] Political propaganda campaigns may be carried out under slogans of "Christ Versus Anti-Christ," or "The Exploited Versus the Exploiters," and the campaigners may, sometimes do, believe in their propaganda, but never so fiercely or determinedly as they proclaim. Carlo Sforza has argued that the Italian *combinazione* is no different from Anglo-Saxon "compromise," but the former is considered wicked and the latter is praised as the height of political wisdom. He blames this on the Italian penchant for discoursing in abstract absolutes, which the British avoid; in the end, opponents come to understandings in both societies.[33] Sforza is wrong. Although the British are not saints, it is possible to reach a compromise between political positions that are not antipathetic without betraying them. Britain has a basically consensual society; Italy has a "fractured" society. The Italian *combinazione* is not the British "compromise," because the Italian deal is not an adjustment between opposing positions within a consensual framework. It is an actual, if not formal, sacrifice of the positions to what Italian society on the whole considers the real objects of politics: power, prestige, and possessions. On these issues, deals are possible. "The typical Italian is anti-ideological—he does not seek change for theoretical reasons—but he is highly realistic." [34]

This realism reflects a fundamental pessimism about human motives and a distrust of popular judgment. Both attitudes contradict, of course, basic assumptions of democracy built into the Constitution of the Italian Republic. Since World War II, political leaders and parties have operated on elitist principles, even when formally committed to equalitarian ones. Clifford A. L. Rich, an acute American observer of postwar political developments, wrote as early as 1949:

A conclusion which seems inevitable to make from a study of Italian political development is that the prevalent theory and practice of governmental and party leadership in Italy is elitist. The concept of the ruling or governing class [*classe dirigente*] is generally accepted by all political groups. . . . The mass followings are regarded as the instruments of power. . . . Both within the party and the state apparatus, democracy implies the ability of contending factions or cliques to impose their predominant leadership and values over the entire organization.[35]

The Christian Democratic Party has played a dominant role in postwar Italian politics. Its outstanding leader was undoubtedly Alcide De Gasperi, who, in a speech in Brussels on November 20, 1948, delivered himself of a few observations on man and the state. He described his point of view as one of "realistic and philosophical pessimism," tempered by the faith that God works not only in individual consciences but also in the life of peoples. Evil is rooted in man. "Unfortunately the root of evil lies in the heart of man who is not only the toy of the '*libido possidenti*' [the drive for possessions] but also of the '*libido dominandi*' of the will to dominate." His political remedy to guarantee liberty and democracy was to set up a system of constitutional checks and balances,* "for you can never adopt optimistic assumptions about the benevolence of men when they possess total power." [36]

Postwar writers have focused their attention on a new elite, the paid professional apparatus of the political parties, the *partitocrazia*. They see the locus of power in the central executive bureaus of the parties. Here is the inner circle, the dictators, the oligarchs who are the final deciders of public policy and the controllers of access to political life.[37]

Ignazio Silone sees in this phenomenon a "Stalinization" of Italian political life spreading from the Communist to the other parties:

Italian political life has been almost completely "Stalinized". . . . Among us, the anti-Communist mass organs have adopted, little by little, the Stalinist system of groups in the apartment houses and in the shops; the fractions of the various party factions are in the unions, the cooperatives, the mutual-aid societies; the party faithful are in the public services, the agitprop men among the crowds; the meetings

---

* De Gasperi himself did nothing about implementing a system of checks and balances while in office. The Constitutional Court, the Regions, and the Superior Council of the Magistrature remained inactivated.

reserved only for the activists, the party schools at all levels of the organization; and that which counts most, and which is essential in Stalinism, the division of the ideology and of the program into two faces, one for the large public, opportunistic and demagogic, the other for the initiates of the central apparatus.[38]

Italian political observers are concerned over the swift degeneration of political institutions in Italy since the early postwar period. Vittorio de Caprariis observes: "There is a degradation of the institutions of liberty and there is a degradation of political society and of all the forces that compose it, not only undeniable but preoccupying, and it speaks for itself." [39] The rise of the *partitocrazia* is considered a major cause of this deleterious phenomenon. Democratic commentators had advocated various measures, such as creating a really effective Constitutional Court (its effectiveness is limited by governmental disregard of its decisions); or eliminating proportional representation and returning to single-member districts. They recognize, however, that these are palliatives rather than remedies, and that democratizing internal party life is the essence of the matter. But even a scholar as democratic in orientation as De Caprariis conceives of democratization primarily as a problem in internal party dynamism involving the mobility of elites and the formation of new ruling groups, based on differences of programs and policies, to offset the bureaucratic sclerosis of the party apparatus.[40] These discussions do not see the involvement of the masses.

Italy does have idealists in the Liberal, Marxist, and Catholic camps and politicians utterly devoted to a cause and to standards of absolute honesty and rectitude. It is not unique in that its political practice leaves much to be desired, but people rarely behave wholly in accordance with the schemes created to analyze their behavior. In Italy, especially, as Borgese notes, reality has softened the sharp outlines of even realistic political analysis:

The hereditary dogmatism of the Italian intelligence had found a countercheck in the equally hereditary and almost instinctive trait of the old nation, which had learned in thousands of years the best lesson of history, namely, that intellectual passions vanish, while benevolence lasts, and that the suggestions of the heart are safer than the pretensions of the mind. This sweetness of Italian life, in spite of poverty and strife, of ecclesiastical and social tyranny, had ever been inspiring to foreigners visiting the country, and it was this rather than imitation of the English parliamentary institutions that made up the particular kind of Italian liberalism which was more psychological than theoretical or political.[41]

"This sweetness of Italian life" is the best way of defining Italian humanism. It has moderated the harshness of the human struggle, tempered De Gasperi's image of man as an amoral competitor, and made supportable the cynicism of his successors.

2

THE POLITICAL AUDIENCE:
COMPOSITION AND
STEREOTYPES

Interest in politics, and in foreign affairs in particular, is usually associated with an advanced level of education and culture. Two qualifications must be made: Many persons with advanced education are uninterested in politics, and some persons who have little education are interested in and attentive to politics.

The general educational level of Italy is relatively low compared to that of other advanced countries. Roughly speaking, the vast majority of the adult population (between 80 and 90 per cent) have had five years of schooling or less. Only a very small proportion of the adult population (between 2 and 3 per cent) are university graduates; larger numbers are graduates of secondary schools (equivalent to United States junior colleges) and junior high schools.

This poor picture must be modified by two important observations: (1) national averages do not reflect regional differences, and the educational picture in the north is much better than in the south; (2) the weight of the past is being overcome by the current rapid expansion of the school population at all educational levels. The youth of the country is staying in school in much larger numbers. Nevertheless, the constitutional requirement of compulsory schooling until the age of fourteen or through junior high school is often honored in the breach, especially in the south.

Given this background, it is not surprising that the reading population is small. Until very recent years, the Italian market for books was extremely limited. However, in the last two or three years purchases of fiction have increased considerably, with a recent best seller, Giuseppe Tomasi di Lampedusa's *The Leopard*, selling more than 200,000 copies. The circulation of light magazines, such as women's magazines, has also expanded.

However, these facts do not indicate the size of the political audience, those persons interested in and attentive to politics; and the international political audience, those attentive to international politics. A sample survey taken in 1958 revealed that 51 per cent of the adult population read daily newspapers, 23 per cent read weeklies, 64 per cent listened to radio news broadcasts, and 23 per cent saw television news programs.[1] Radio and television news is given in fifteen-minute narrative-descriptive reports, with little or no interpretation. In 1960, a half-hour political program was inaugurated on television. Called "Tribuna politica," it consisted of interviews of leading politicians. In other words, obtaining the news only from radio and television hardly indicates any substantial interest in or attention to politics.

A minimal requirement is regular reading of the political news in the newspapers. Higher standards would demand the reading of news magazines; even higher, of specialized journals or books. Let us consider the minimal standard, newspaper reading. The adults who claim to read newspapers do not necessarily read the political news with any regularity, but perhaps turn rather directly to the sports and human-interest pages. No figures are available on the proportion of newspaper readers who read the political news. Guesses made by journalists in conversation with me ranged from a minimum 1 per cent (the estimate of a diplomatic correspondent) to 5 per cent (the estimate of a correspondent specializing in national politics). Journalists, however, tend toward cynicism, so perhaps we might double these figures.

That the readership of the political reporters is small can be deduced from the style and nature of their reporting. Their writing is full of nuances and subtleties, indicative of the level of their audience. A comment by Enzo Forcella, a nationally known political reporter, is illustrative:

A political journalist in our country can count on about 1,500 readers: the ministers and the undersecretaries (all), the parliamentarians (part), the party leaders, trade-union leaders, high prelates, and a few industrialists who want to appear informed. The rest do not count, even if the paper sells 300,000 copies. First of all, it has not been ascertained that the ordinary readers read the first pages of the papers, and in any case their influence is minimal. The entire system is organized on the relation between the political journalist and this group of privileged readers. Overlooking this element, one cuts oneself off from understanding the most characteristic aspect of our political journalism, maybe of Italian politics: it is the atmosphere of the play within the family, with protagonists who have known each other from childhood, who make cracks in each other's presence, who speak an allusive language, and who, even when they detest each other, love each other.[2]

This cynical description of the political act, the role of the journalist, and the limited audience is exaggerated for emphasis. Yet it is basically true. In foreign affairs, the audience is even smaller, and the number of political actors more restricted. International concerns seem even more remote from daily life than national issues, in spite of the atomic and hydrogen bombs. The decline of Italy as a power, with the resultant feeling of helplessness, has induced even the politically conscious intellectual to ignore events beyond the borders, unless they are of a spectacular nature. Spacemen and the Berlin wall do get notice, as does a summit meeting. But such sporadic attention does not provide the basis for accurate and informed judgments.

Of course, Italy is not too different from other countries in this respect. The United States, with the world's most advanced general educational system and an extensive distribution of mass-communication media, differs only to a limited degree. A recent investigation revealed that about 10 per cent of the American people demonstrated a strong interest in world affairs and that only a small proportion of the "community leaders" devoted much attention to international issues or the United Nations.[3]

The general indifference to politics is accentuated among the women. A survey of women disclosed that 52 per cent of them believed it was wrong for a woman to be interested in politics and to have political opinions. Among those who felt that women should be interested in politics, the majority voted for the left-wing parties, Communist and Socialist; among those who felt that women should not be interested in politics, the majority voted for the Christian Democratic and right-wing parties.[4] There are more female than male voters in Italy (in the 1958 election, 16,931,263 women voted and 15,576,076 men), and the women support the Christian Democratic Party far more strongly than the men do,[5] and are much more impressed by monarchy and aristocracy than the men are.[6] This indicates that the postwar governments, centered on the Christian Democratic Party and, until recently, generally supported by the Right, have had little popular opinion to guide or control their policies and, conversely, little responsibility to their own electorate. This indifference to political issues among large segments of the Christian Democratic electorate extends to the power struggles within the party. A poll of Christian Democratic voters was made by Doxa, the public-opinion agency, in the spring of 1958, at the peak of the election campaign. The subjects were asked: "According to your viewpoint, in the interests of the country, which currents and which men would it be desirable to have prevail within the Christian Democratic Party?" The results are shown in Table 1.

This indifference to broader issues is not confined to the electorate of the Christian Democratic Party. Furthermore, it is not limited to the electorate but pervades the lower levels of party organization. Turning again to the Socialist Party, we have the following picture:

The base of the party . . . participates very slightly in political discussions in the true sense, contenting itself with affirmations of faith in socialism and deprecating the struggles of the various factions, which are considered unpropitious for unity and harmony among Socialists. The leaders, whether they be functionaries or elected officeholders, are the only ones to concern themselves with politics in the true sense, which thereby becomes an encounter and a clash at the summit, leaving the base more or less indifferent. . . . On a higher level, on the key themes of general policy, only a few groups are engaged: parliamentarians (not all), a few communal and provincial councilors, functionaries of the federations, and small nuclei of young intellectuals, who have become members of the party relatively recently.[7]

In this kind of situation, major decisions can be—and often must be—taken without any base in a popular consensus. The single most

TABLE 1

ATTITUDES OF CHRISTIAN DEMOCRATIC SYMPATHIZERS

	Per 100 Voters
Current	
Left or Center-Left	4
Center	4
Right or Center-Right	4
Other answers regarding currents or tendencies	1
Persons	
Pella	5
Fanfani	3
Other answers regarding persons	4
Other Answers	
I am indifferent, I take no interest in those things	20
I am in no position to answer	62
TOTAL	107*

* The total exceeds 100 because some respondents gave more than one answer.
Source: *L'Espresso* (Rome), May 4, 1958, p. 7.

important foreign-policy decision made by a postwar Italian government was to join the Western alliance system, the North Atlantic Treaty Organization. Count Sforza, then Foreign Minister, later wrote to his Ambassador in Washington, Alberto Tarchiani: "I guided our foreign policy, in the midst of innumerable obstacles, on the path to the West, to the Atlantic alliance and the European community, with the full and faithful approval and cooperation of the Prime Minister [De Gasperi] and the Cabinet, even if often with little comprehension or scarce appreciation from the great public." [8] Yet Sforza often found it convenient to use the fiction of a mass public opinion forcing him to follow a certain line. In 1948, he justified an Italian claim to regain Eritrea on the ground that public opinion would react strongly to abandoning the old colony.[9] Of course, no such reaction occurred when the colony was lost.

Professor Renzo Sereno has written: "Italians like movies, soccer, and girls. Politics are of little interest and foreign affairs even less." [10] This does not mean that the general population does not have a mass of prejudices and preferences, antipathies and attractions, which affect the mood and *milieu* of the country. They have attitudes toward what is going on in the world even if their information is often inaccurate. The political or the ruling class cannot be immune to these moods, which condition, if not control, the concrete decisions that may be made. Let us now turn to some of these antipathies and preferences.

A few words must be written about Italian nationalism. The Italians' consciousness of their identity as a distinct group is very old. It antedates modern nationalism and the political state called Italy.[11] Its basis is cultural, not political (although the Italians themselves make invidious distinctions about the cultural patterns of the various regions of the country). A real political identification, if it exists, is more likely to be with a historic commune. These ancient loyalties persist, despite a hundred years of patriotic indoctrination through a nationalized educational system. (Of course, relatively few Italians have gone through the system for any length of time.)

Italian cultural nationalism tends toward chauvinism, with repeated references to the heritage of a "plurimillenary civilization" and the "primacy" of Italy's past. These chauvinists would be hard put to point to such a primacy today, but do claim that "everyone recognizes our primacy in the artistic and cultural fields." [12] The modern Italian state operates at a terrible disadvantage under this burden; nothing it does can compare with the achievements of the past. Little wonder that its own citizens are so contemptuous of it.

Thus, Italians can identify with other Italians, but not with Italy. They can exult or suffer over the victories or defeats of Italian soccer teams or beauty queens engaged in international competition. But few of them would die for Italy. This indifference is perhaps even greater today than in the recent past because of the absence of an aura of legitimacy about present political institutions, and the decline of idealism since the struggle for liberation.

As attitudes toward one's own country affect its international power position, so attitudes toward foreign countries may affect relations with those countries. Like other peoples, the Italians can acquire preferences or antipathies for foreign nations, based at times on experience, at other times on propaganda. Various opinion surveys made in the Cold War period have revealed the United States as the most-liked, and Russia as the most-disliked foreign state, with the attitude partly reversed among the partisans of the extreme Left.* A persistent, deep-seated antagonism is felt toward England, and to a somewhat lesser degree toward France. A Doxa survey in November, 1953, inquired which of four countries—the United States, England, France, and Germany—was liked best. Only 3 per cent put England first and 47 per cent put it last; 12 per cent put France first and 4 per cent last; 22 per cent put Germany first and 20 per cent last; 56 per cent put the United States first and 6 per cent last.[13] At the same time, it was found that more of those interviewed thought England had been more hostile than Russia to Italy since the end of the war. (The figures were 41 per cent and 37 per cent respectively, with the remainder "don't knows.")[14] The neo-Fascists of the Movimento Sociale Italiano were more anti-British than anti-Russian.[15] But this opinion is not necessarily limited to the extreme Right. Luzzatto Fegiz has written: "The single point of agreement among the Italians seems to be, in fact . . . the decided antipathy for the English found among all social classes and all political currents." [16]

We have here a residue of Mussolini's influence, dating back to the Ethiopian war and the League of Nations sanctions. These antagonisms have been nurtured by postwar troubles over the African colonies and, more importantly, over Trieste (for which the Italians tended to blame the British, who dominated the Anglo-American occupation force in Zone A of the Free Territory of Trieste). They have found expression in a kind of pro-Arabism, which is in many cases a camouflage for anti-British sentiment.[17] An outright anti-British, anti-French explosion occurred in 1956 over the fiasco of the Anglo-French-Israeli attack on Egypt. Italy had been driven out of Africa and thwarted in the Middle East by Britain and, to a lesser extent, France, and so the Italian intelligentsia of nearly all political persuasions took great pleasure in seeing Britain and France similarly

* The reversal is only partial because the opinion polls reveal that a considerable percentage of Communist respondents bear no dislike for the United States and are not overly enraptured by Russia.

frustrated. France's troubles in Algeria stimulated open joy among Italians whose parties plumped for Atlantic solidarity and the European community.

It is difficult to evaluate the Fascist impact on the Italian mood. Rome is probably the most Fascist city in Italy. It is filled with aged bureaucrats brought there to swell the administrative machine of the Fascist state. The newsstands are piled with dailies and weeklies running feature stories recalling the days of Fascism, Nazism, and the monarchy. An informal sampling of newsstands during the late spring of 1959 revealed the following headlines in nationally distributed periodicals:

A THOUSAND ANECDOTES ABOUT MUSSOLINI (*Oggi*)
THE SON OF THE BLACKSMITH (*Tempo*)
GOEBBELS' DIARY (*Rotosei*)
THE TRUTH ABOUT HITLER'S WOMEN (*Gente*)
EDDA AND RACHELE: MEMOIRS OF VITTORIO MUSSOLINI (*Epoca*)
HUMBERT OF SAVOY SPEAKS OF MUSSOLINI AND OF HIS FATHER, THE KING (*Settimana incom*)
A FEATURE BY PAULA HITLER: MY BROTHER ADOLF (*Tempo illustrato*)
DINO GRANDI TELLS WHAT HE HAS ALWAYS HIDDEN (*Oggi*)[18]

It is questionable whether all this should be taken seriously. There is a market for this material; some of these journals have wide circulations, although not necessarily because of these feature stories. To offset this influence, there has been a successful revival after 1959 of anti-Fascist movies and novels.

The dominant fact of international life since the late 1940's has been the Cold War. Italy has been the most loyal of U.S. allies in its foreign policy. Nonetheless, among 100 people polled by Doxa, the blame for the Cold War was assigned as shown in Table 2. Nor do most Italians accept the U.S. explanation that the Cold War is caused by Russia's drive to dominate the world. Important segments of the Italian population (from 33 per cent to 52 per cent), spread among various parties, believed that both the U.S. and the U.S.S.R. wanted to dominate the world.[19] The question, "Does

America want to dominate the world?," produced this distribution of opinion:

	Per Cent
True	29
Partly true	40
False	23
No answer	8
	100

Most of the anti-Americans were found among the extreme Left and the neo-Fascists.[20] Undoubtedly part of this anti-American sentiment springs from domestic politics. Identification of the United States with certain Italian parties and institutions, such as the Christian Democrats and the Vatican, for example, tends to push anti-clericals into the anti-American camp. Identification of the United States with Italian big-business interests may incline left-wing Christian Democrats who support the state-owned concerns toward an anti-American position.

TABLE 2

ASSIGNMENT OF RESPONSIBILITY FOR TWO-BLOC WORLD

Cause	
United States	12
Russia	27
England	5
United States and Russia	26
Capitalists	6
Communists	4
The allies	1
Other answers	3
Don't know	21
TOTAL	105

* The total exceeds 100 because some respondents gave more than one answer.
Source: Luzzatto Fegiz, *Il volto sconosciuto,* p. 739.

Of course, the Italians who think that America wants to dominate the world may not consider this objective either likely or unnatural. Italians consider it quite natural to seek power, to want to dominate (what De Gasperi called the *libido dominandi*), so it is not surprising that Italians attribute this motivation to American policy.

The general population may also have opinions on Italian foreign policy, even though these are not founded on any consistent, penetrating attention. Most Italians have gradually become aware that Italy is part of a Western alliance system. This is the fundamental fact of Italian foreign policy, yet surveys have revealed that there is

TABLE 3

ATTITUDES TOWARD ITALY'S SECURITY

(In Per Cents)

	General Public	Upper Group (Political Class)
To continue present arrangements for Western defense based on the alliance with the Western countries and the U.S.	33	49
To form an alliance limited to Western European countries	4	12
To arrange a general security system that would include the U.S., Russia, and other European nations	18	26
To withdraw from all alliances and take a position of neutrality	21	7
Other	1	—
Don't know	23	6
TOTALS	100	100

Source: Lloyd A. Free and Renzo Sereno, *Italy: Dependent Ally or Independent Partner?* (Princeton, N.J.: Institute for International Social Research, 1957), p. 121.

no firm majority behind it. In December, 1955, a representative sample of two groups was asked, "Under present circumstances, which do you think is the most practical way for Italy to ensure its security?" The responses appear in Table 3.

In 1958, there was some awareness that American long-range-missile bases might be established in Italy and that proposals had been made looking toward some sort of disengagement in Central Europe. Sample surveys of opinion were made on both questions. The results are given in Table 4.

TABLE 4

ATTITUDES TOWARD MISSILE BASES AND DISENGAGEMENT

(*In Per Cents*)

Question: Do you favor establishment of long-range-missile bases by the U.S.?

	Favor	Oppose	Don't Know	Depends
Total Sample	30	39	29	2
By Education Level				
Primary education or less	25	39	34	2
Secondary education	39	39	19	3
Superior, university	48	33	15	4

* * *

Question: If Russia offered to withdraw forces from East Germany, Poland, and Czechoslovakia, should the U.S., Britain, and France accept the Russian offer and withdraw their forces from West Germany?

	Favor	Oppose	Don't Know	Depends
Total Sample	53	12	27	8
By Educational Level				
Primary education or less	52	9	34	5
Secondary education	62	17	10	11
Superior, university	50	21	11	18

Source: Polls taken in March, 1958, by the *Istituto italiano dell' opinione pubblica*.

The Italian Government agreed to the American missile bases, and they have already been constructed and are in operation. In 1958 and for some time thereafter, the Italian Government opposed any kind of disengagement in any form (including the Rapacki plan for nuclear disengagement in Central Europe).

Questions can be raised concerning the validity or significance of the polls reported above. Some of the sympathies and antipathies revealed may be transient, caused by events of the moment. Probably many of the respondents did not understand the issues about which they were being questioned. Most of these polls were taken in the 1950's; rapid economic development at the end of that decade helped to increase educational levels and, perhaps, the level of political attention. Certain specific antipathies, such as the one against England, have probably declined. In 1962, the Italian Government strongly desired to bring England into the European Common Market to help offset the weight of the De Gaulle-Adenauer diarchy. Deep-seated attitudes change very slowly, however, and stereotypes fade only after long intervals of time. These inquiries provide whatever material is available, and we have to use them even when recognizing their limitations. They indicate that broad opinion has little direct influence on government policy. Yet, in modern times, no government can have an effective foreign policy without mass support. The Italian people were brought into two world wars in the twentieth century, once by a liberal government and once by a dictator. The large masses were indifferent or opposed. The consequences are writ large in the history of Italy.

3

HISTORIC ENDS AND MEANS IN ITALIAN FOREIGN POLICY

Giuseppe Borgese has vividly described the Roman imperial cancer that affected the Italian intelligentsia from 1870 on. The preceding centuries of foreign domination had created Italian complexes of inferiority and despair,[1] which led, on one hand, to unceasing self-abasement and, on the other, after unity was finally realized and Rome was now the capital, to grandiose expectations. The big dispute in Italy in the 1870's and 1880's was not over whether Italy should be a great imperial power, but over whether it already was one in fact and not just in name. The historic Left thought it already was one in fact, the historic Right thought it had a long way to go, and saw the first job as building up Italy internally.[2] From 1870 on, Renato Giordano observes:

. . . Italy was divided between the supporters of a moderate, dignified, policy, aware of the limitations of our possibilities—the policy that is, of the historic Right, of Visconti-Venosta and later of Giolitti— and the advocates of an audacious, or rather fearful, policy of colonial conquests and military grandeur, the policy of Crispi and of Sonnino, the policy of the nationalists. The first knew that the *porro unum* of the new Italian state was international peace and they therefore identified the interests of Italy with the stability of the European political concert. In particular, friendship with Great Britain became the undisputed principle of our Ministry of Foreign Affairs . . . the nationalists, instead, and their precursors dreamed of a modern Rome (a third Rome), that would equal the grandeur of the Rome of the Caesars; they venerated the power and the style of Prussian militarism, they incited [Italians] to strategic expansion in the Mediterranean and in Africa, to the creation of a great military and colonial power. On the mounting wave of such sentiments, Crispi embarked on the Abyssinian adventure and Mussolini launched, in effect, tragically, his bellicose pseudo-imperialistic experiments.[3]

After 1876, the historic Left was in power until the end of the century. Its goals were the *grandezza* (grandeur) of the fatherland and diplomatic supremacy in the Mediterranean. Italy entered the Triple Alliance in 1882 for prestige, to reinforce a domestic position and to escape from international isolation.[4] To Crispi, especially, the chief objective of foreign policy was prestige.[5] Mussolini, also, was driven by the thirst for glory and prestige. In the Italian tradition, the Rome of the Caesars provides the ultimate measure of achievement. So it is not surprising that in the 1930's the "call of Rome" became the central focus of Fascist policy.[6] Pride of culture made it necessary to pursue the emigrants, who had been abandoning Italy in ever larger numbers since 1880, to their new homelands in a losing struggle to preserve their *italianità*.[7]

These expansionist objectives were fostered by the military atmosphere of the royal court. Victor Emmanuel II was always surrounded by the military and rarely wore civilian clothes. War was regarded as a gentlemanly and desirable occupation. Until the turn of the century, military officers were at the head of the War and Navy departments; like all other officers, they swore a personal oath of loyalty to the King. Wars were entered into lightheartedly, when Italy was unprepared to fight, in 1895, in 1911, in 1915 (and in 1940).[8] The economy was crushed by extravagant military expenditures, several times without parliamentary sanction. In 1901, Italy was spending 40 per cent of the state budget for military purposes; between 1860 and 1940, well over a third of state expenditures was allocated for war.[9] The growing economic protectionism at the end of the nineteenth century, the subsidization of uneconomic heavy industries, was a result of this effort by Italy to be a power among the powers, to do what the others were doing. It reached its extreme in Mussolini's policy of autarchy, but it was not originated by Fascism. Likewise, the glorification of war, so antipathetic to the humanistic segment of Italian tradition, antedates Fascism.

Economic motives, although not dominant, did play a role in historic Italian foreign policy. Italy put a tremendous effort into contracting trade treaties. On occasion, it would endanger basic political policies in the thirst for profits. Once Italy even threatened not to renew the Triple Alliance unless commercial favors were granted.[10] But sentimental egoism rather than materialism appears, on the whole, to have been the predominant drive.

The emphasis on armed forces and the uneven development of the economy to support them did not, of course, cure Italy's fundamental economic and political weakness and transform her into a European power. The wiser Italian statesmen and professional diplomats recognized this. Ever since Cavour, the basis of Italian foreign policy had been to compensate for Italy's weakness by exploiting the rivalries of the other powers.[11] In consequence, Italian foreign policy was inevitably unstable. Its vacillation is best exemplified, perhaps, in the Prinetti-Barrère exchange of notes in 1902, which served to nullify Italian commitments under the Triple Alliance.[12] Baron Raffaele Guariglia, a career diplomat, commented in 1932 that Italy was "historically constrained, for intrinsic and obvious reasons, to take its stand first on one side and then the other; to pursue the execution of its aims by cutting from the garments of its different adversaries the material necessary for its own cloak; and to take refuge on rainy days (so long as this cloak was not ready) under the ample and capacious mantle of England." [13]

Mussolini, mistakenly thinking the cloak was ready, abandoned England's capacious mantle, and even sought to destroy it. A shrewder predecessor, Giovanni Giolitti, sheltered himself not only in England's mantle, but in the rest of Europe's as well, and took Libya in 1911 and 1912 with the acquiescence of all the powers.[14] The Duce, when he relieved Dino Grandi as Foreign Minister in 1931 and sent him off to London as Ambassador, complained that Grandi "had made Italian policy deviate from the straight course of egoism and realism and compromised the aspirations of a new generation." [15]

This historic penchant for straddling alignments is not explained solely by Italy's weak position on the international scene. It was also a product of the "transformist" character of domestic Italian politics, in which a change in position was common in the scramble for honors and perquisites. Until the Italian Socialist Party was founded, before the turn of the century, there were no parties with a program based on a philosophy of society and the state. Instead, there were shifting groups attached to individuals whose manipulations and deals constituted the governmental process. But not even the Socialist Party was immune from personalism.[16] So it would be strange indeed if foreign policy were viewed as totally different, subject to other rules of behavior. Italy's weakness, combined with a desire for glory and increased power and wealth, would strongly induce the transference of domestic patterns to the international scene. When Prime Minister Antonio Salandra reversed Italy's alliances in 1915 and brought the country into the Triple Entente, he justified his move with the phrase "sacred egoism." The same slogan could just as well have rationalized the domestic political behavior of the *trasformisti*.

The hierarchical pattern of Italian society after unification, the personalism of the business and political worlds, the strong oligarchical leadership, were carried to extremes in foreign policy. From 1870 to the turn of the century, foreign policy was effectively immune to public opinion—that is, the opinions of the political class, not the masses. Foreign policy was rarely debated in Parliament. When it was, the discussion was usually perfunctory. The King played a direct and often dominant role in such matters. The important decisions were made by him in conjunction with a few ministers, key diplomats stationed at the major capitals, and high Foreign Office functionaries.[17] Sometimes the King conducted a policy independent of, even contrary to, that of the Prime Minister.[18] The Foreign Minister was often the King's personal choice, and when the King and Foreign Minister cooperated, it was quite possible for them to ignore the rest of the government and Parliament. In the first decade of the twentieth century, parliamentary and public discussion of foreign policy increased somewhat. The Socialist Party opposed Italy's membership in the Triple Alliance, and a rising irredentism influenced other parties—including the Republican and Radical (actually, they were more like groups than parties)—against Italy's allies. Nevertheless Giolitti and his Foreign Minister, with the King's approval, ignored the parliamentary and press discussion and renewed the Triple Alliance.[19]

At the outbreak of World War I, Italy immediately declared its neutrality, based on Austria-Hungary's violations of the terms of the Triple Alliance. However, Foreign Minister Di San Giuliano (who died in October, 1914) hinted that, in return for sufficient compensation, Italy might fight with its allies. The subsequent public debate between neutralists and interventionists on the side of the Triple Entente showed that intervention was opposed by a large majority among the masses and in Parliament,[20] where the neutralist Giolitti, not in the government, still dominated the parliamentary majority. Intervention was opposed by the Socialists, the Vatican, and large sections of the political class. (The peasants and workers could not have cared less.) Yet, without the knowledge of the rest of the Cabinet or of the General Staff, King Victor Emmanuel III, his Prime Minister, Antonio Salandra, and his Foreign Minister, Sydney Sonnino, proceeded to negotiate the Treaty of London with the Triple Entente nations. Meanwhile, Parliament was not called into session. After the treaty had been signed, Parliament was convened, and on May 20, 1915, Mack Smith writes, "Under severe intimidation, forsaken by their leader, Giolitti, and knowing now the extent of the King's involvement, the deputies gave the government full powers 'in case of war' by 407 votes to 74." [21] The Socialists voted No. The circumstances under which Italy entered the war partially explain its performance during most of the subsequent three and one-half years. They do more. They demonstrate the breakdown of effective parliamentary government in Italy, and its resultant final collapse after the war.

In the light of this history and of the nature of a totalitarian regime, it is not surprising that there were few restrictions on foreign-policy decisions under Fascism. After Fascism fell, it became the custom to blame everything on Mussolini. In their memoirs, most of his collaborators denied having any effective influence on him. Decision-making between 1922 and 1943 is often described in terms of the tragic will of one man, the supine acquiescence of the few around him, all of whom claimed to serve the fatherland but in reality served only themselves.[22] Even Winston Churchill supported this picture, describing Italy's entry into World War II on June 10, 1940, as the product of the Duce's will. "One man and one man alone . . . against the Crown and the Royal Family of Italy, against the Pope and all the authority of the Vatican and of the Roman

Catholic Church, against the wishes of the Italian people . . . has arrayed the trustees and inheritors of ancient Rome upon the side of the ferocious pagan barbarians." [23]

There is little evidence that the people, or the Church, or the King directly affected the decisions that swept Italy to disaster. But there is little evidence that they tried to affect them. The masses, of course, could not be expected to. The conciliation between Church and State took place in February, 1929; in 1935, the Vatican indirectly, and many members of the Italian ecclesiastical hierarchy directly, supported the Ethiopian adventure. The Vatican openly supported Mussolini's intervention in the Spanish Civil War. There is little evidence that it acted energetically to preserve Italian neutrality in World War II.[24] Even if it had, it could not have succeeded.

Victor Emmanuel III reveled in being Emperor of Ethiopia and King of Albania. He signed the declaration of war against France and England. Under the *Statuto albertino*, it was the King who declared war. Perhaps he had no choice, but in that case he had no power, and his lack of authority was the result of mistakes he had made over the years.

The generals and the business groups might be considered as potential sources of restraint, but there is no evidence that in fact they were. Pietro Badoglio, Chief of the High Command, still defended the Ethiopian expedition in the memoirs he wrote after everything had collapsed. He claimed he tried to deter the decision to attack France,[25] but this claim must be viewed with suspicion. The generals and their King, like many others, apparently thought that the Germans had won the war by June, 1940, and that a quick march was all that would be required of Italy before the division of the spoils.

The business groups as a whole were the major supporters and beneficiaries of the regime, but there is little evidence that they were interested or influential in grand policy. They exploited the drive for autarchy and benefited from the military expenditures, but, the incomplete evidence indicates, they primarily tended to business.*

---

* During the latter part of World War II, Marshal Caviglia of the Italian General Staff made the following observation: "The Italian bourgeoisie is rotten. The bourgeoisie is guided and attracted exclusively by its own interests, is only interested in enrichment, thinks of nothing else, works for nothing else. Today it is hiding and trying not to work for the Germans, not because of a belief, but

Another potential influence on Mussolini was the career diplomats. In the early years after the march on Rome, holdovers from pre-Fascist days—such as Contarini, Secretary-General of the Foreign Office, and Barone, Director-General of Political Affairs—served as something of a moderating influence. Their most effective deterrent to a rash action was to warn the Duce that it would make him look ridiculous, for Mussolini was extremely sensitive about his *bella figura*.[26] Italian career diplomats were generally apolitical, i.e., conservative and nationalistic. They were not opposed to the Duce's political philosophy. They, too, wanted to see Italy great and prestigious, enlarged in territory and influence. But they were more patient, moderate, and realistic.[27] Unlike him, they did not glorify war. Their influence declined in 1925, when Mussolini, then also Foreign Minister, began to work behind Contarini's back in dealing with Yugoslavia.[28] When Dino Grandi was made Foreign Minister, their influence increased, as he appeared amenable to their suggestions. Then Mussolini began circumventing Grandi. Mussolini personally conducted the negotiations with the Vatican that led to the Lateran Treaties of 1929. Grandi knew nothing about them.[29] Finally, Mussolini got rid of Grandi, because he was insufficiently "egoistic and realistic."

In the early 1930's, the career diplomats agreed with Mussolini that the rift among the great powers gave Italy the chance to realize her African aspirations. The Foreign Office officials actively helped prepare for the Abyssinian war.[30] When Count Galeazzo Ciano, the Duce's son-in-law, was made Foreign Minister, he made increased prestige and power his principal objectives.[31] He soon reduced the traditional Foreign Office apparatus to an empty shell, using instead his personal cabinet, which he expanded enormously. Decisions were made from above. Official channels were bypassed; the diplomats were not asked for advice or recommendations.[32]

The decrease in the role of the professionals was not necessarily accompanied by an increase in the role of the Fascist Party hierarchs. In 1928, Mussolini foisted a number of party hacks onto the Foreign

only because it feels that the Germans will soon be gone and the Americans will be coming. It is formed of straw dogs who go wherever there is a bone to eat, and as soon as they smell danger or a change in the situation, they hide." Quoted in Angelo Magliano, *La borghesia e la paura* (Florence: Vallechi, 1957), p. 47.

Office, but the professionals largely succeeded in assigning them to minor positions, especially in the consular service.[33] Grandi and Ciano were both party men, but neither appears to have been greatly impressed with fellow members of the Fascist Grand Council, the highest party organ. If a pro-German faction developed in the party in the late 1930's, Mussolini was the head of it and Ciano a charter member. Occasionally, they became nervous about or irritated at their Nazi ally, but not until the world was at the threshold of catastrophe did they have second thoughts. In August, 1939, after meeting with Von Ribbentrop at Salzburg, Ciano woke up to what was happening and became converted to an anti-German policy. The Duce was never converted.[34] He grudgingly declared Italy a non-belligerent in September, because of his awareness of Italy's weakness. He happily intervened in the war as soon as it looked safe to do so. Other Fascist hierarchs had little effect on his decisions.

Thus the dominant themes in Italian foreign policy for most of the period from 1870 to World War II are summed up in Mussolini's phrase "egoism and realism." Egoism defined the goals, realism the means. In foreign policy, egoism placed prestige and glory before material gain, reversing the priority of the peasants and even the gentry, whose opportunities for glory were almost nil. Until Mussolini and Ciano died, the pursuers of glory had not directly paid its price, for the economic burdens of Italian foreign policy fell on the poor, because of the protectionism given to industry and because of a regressive system of indirect taxation.

The egoism of the goals, however, interfered with the realism of the means, resulting in successive failures in evaluating Italy's relative power position and capabilities. Crispi and Mussolini made the most noticeable mistakes, but not the only ones. The intense desire to belong to the truly great too often led to humiliation, which in turn led to tragic domestic consequences and created unusual sensitivity to questions of prestige in foreign affairs.[35]

Yet this unattractive picture is somewhat overdrawn. Italian imperialism prior to World War I was little different from that of its European contemporaries, even if somewhat more strident and operating from a weaker base. Not all Italian statesmen prior to Mussolini miscalculated, and even he was not always wrong. Not all were merely egoists and crafty realists. The Risorgimento saw much idealism, and not all of it disappeared in 1870. Mazzini and Garibaldi were idealists and eventually failed in their dreams of creating a united, republican, and democratic Italy through popular and spontaneous action. But the unified monarchical and liberal Italy created by 1870 cannot be explained merely by the egoism of the kings of the House of Savoy or the crafty realism of Count Cavour. There was more than that to Piedmont's policies.

After 1870, some politicians saw that Italy needed peace to develop and recognized that Italy's best contribution to peace was to help maintain the European balance of power, not to upset it. Such men turned down the opportunity to participate in the imperialist expansion into Egypt in 1882. Later, when imperialism became a more dominant mirage before their eyes, they saw that Italy's imperial action helped contribute to, rather than undermine, the European balance worked out in Africa.

Nor were all the interventionists in the 1914–15 debate blinded by the attractions of "sacred egoism." An interventionist minority looked upon Italy's entry into the war as the final completion of the Risorgimento, the bringing into the motherland of the last "unredeemed" territories. Democratic interventionists such as Leonida Bissolati and Gaetano Salvemini argued that the Triple Entente was defending freedom and democracy in Europe (Czarist Russia was a long way off) against autocratic Prussian domination of the Continent.[36] Under Fascism, however, such voices were stilled.

Thus, idealism has not been absent in modern Italian foreign policy, but it has not predominated. Contemporary Italy, the Italy of the 1950's and 1960's, is very much the heir of the dominant tradition. Egoism and realism are still very much to the fore.

However, the stakes are couched in the most moralistic and idealistic terms. Both Cold War and domestic political struggles are usually presented in terms of Christ versus anti-Christ, humanism versus barbarism, conceptions of life that are fundamentally incompatible, etc. The Christian Democrats, who have dominated Italian political life since the end of World War II, have used these themes generously. In a speech to the U.S. Congress, President Gronchi defined international relations in the following language:

In almost the entire world, two fundamental conceptions confront each other in the life of modern nations: the state for the individual or the individual for the state? Western democracy, that is, freedom, or people's democracy, that is, Marxist-Leninist? An ideology such as the latter, organically antithetic to ours both as a moral and a social conception, has a great force of expansion in itself since it appears to represent a political and social system capable of liberating the most disinherited classes from their inferiority and their misery.[37]

Defining international politics as a struggle between opposing moral systems is not confined to the Christian Democrats. On June 17, 1958, after listening to a loud hue and cry in the Chamber of Deputies over the Hungarian Government's execution of the rebel leaders Nagy and Maleter, Pietro Ingrao, of the executive bureau of the Italian Communist Party, rose and replied, "This is a struggle between your world and ours. You don't cry when Communists are shot." [38]

Despite these statements, the real situation appears to be quite different. The moralists among Christian Democrats, Communists, and others are a tiny minority. It has been shown in earlier chapters that the over-all Italian attitude toward politics is nonideological. We can recall De Gasperi's cynical and pessimistic reflections upon the *libido dominandi* and the *libido possidendi*, and remind ourselves that these conclusions are based as much on close and long association with members of his own party and faith, as on a knowledge of others outside either or both. We can remember that large-scale voting shifts from Christian Democratic to Communist parties or vice versa are primarily a product of local and immediate material gains and losses for the voters involved.

A moralistic approach toward international politics appears incongruous with domestic politics. Italians look at political facts with a certain detachment, the product of a very ancient civil experience.[39] The very same Christian Democrats can talk about the necessity of "reconciling divergent opinions," and at the same time describe Italy's foreign policy as a "defense of a centuries-old civilization against an ideology and form of existence" that can never be tolerated.[40] President Gronchi, speaking at the United Nations, defined its fundamental task as the "reciprocal narrowing of the distance, through fecund discussion, with the intention of bringing the governments together again";[41] earlier he had said that this distance existed because the Marxist-Leninist way of life was "organically antithetic to ours both as a moral and a social conception." The attitude depends on which audience one is addressing. The fact remains that organically antithetic conceptions cannot be synthesized or "reconciled." The official organ of the Christian Democratic Party, *Il Popolo*, once found it necessary to counter Communist attacks by declaring in an editorial that NATO's leaders "are not inspired by bellicose hatred and by ideological wrath," that divergences exist but are solved by discussion, with full respect for the other side's views.[42] An anonymous but authoritative writer defined Communist and Russian imperialism as the same thing, which destroys its ideological content.[43]

Italian politicians look upon international politics with utter realism. Former Foreign Minister Gaetano Martino described international politics in this way:

> Now there is no doubt that international politics, more than other politics, is a *Realpolitik*. . . . *Realpolitik* is the experience of everyone who in the social world in which he is called upon to live behaves knowing exactly on whom and on what he can count in putting into practice the program of his life. . . . The social world of the nations is the international world. If foreign policy has a tradition of crude realism, that has depended and in part still depends on the characteristics of such a society in which the weight of force prevails ever more over the rule of law. . . . International politics has been and is still held, more than the others, to be conditioned by reality, that is by the relation of forces, which is not a subjective but an objective fact.[44]

The "relation of forces," the balance of power—on these concepts Italian political thinking is built. The concept of equilibrium is central; journalists, professors, politicians, professional diplomats—they all use it. They use it loosely. There are two variations. In one, equilibrium is a situation of checks and balances, in which independent forces prevent one another from becoming dominant and destroying the others' independence. In the second, equilibrium is a stable power relationship. The situation is in balance; nothing is changing. But it gets out of balance when power positions begin to shift. A stable totalitarian dictatorship will be in equilibrium although no independent internal forces exist to check its power. It gets out of equilibrium when such forces arise to challenge it.

Thus, international conflict is seen as the result not of incompatible moral worlds, but of a rupture of equilibrium. In the words of Count Massimo Magistrati, the former Director-General of Political Affairs in the Foreign Office, it is the "disequilibrium of force . . . which is and always will be—as history clearly teaches—the principal cause of international contrasts and conflicts." [45]

Mario Toscano, the diplomatic historian, has expanded on the components of equilibrium in modern times:

> It is commonly held that domestic and international peace derive from a balance of power. This balance, legally fixed by treaties on the international level and by constitutions on the domestic plane, is susceptible to change in proportion to the dynamics of the economic, military, political, social, ideological, moral, and religious forces composing it. When the factors producing any given juridical crystallization assume such proportions as to render the existing order completely inadequate and ineffective, the balance is broken and, through various procedures (be they pacific or violent), its material reconstruction and the resultant new legal framework are made necessary. This phenomenon in the history of international relations is generally illustrated by the theory of the balance of power, considered in a positive sense, which is to say in relation to the ability of the individual powers to promote changes in it.[46]

He recognizes that ideological, moral, and religious factors may affect the international balance and are components of it, but does not claim they are inevitable causes of conflict. He observes that incompatible ideological and moral systems have lived peacefully with each other in the past and can do so in the future, without formally renouncing their principles, as long as an effective balance is maintained.[47]

Italian proponents of European federation argue that it would create a more articulated balance of power than the precarious equilibrium of two hostile colossi. Most of them reject a "third force" position as premature now but see it as an eventual means of escaping "subjection" to an American sphere of influence.[48]

Moralists do exist. However, they do not all see the conflict in the same light. More true moralists are found among small groups of secularist intellectuals than among most Christian Democrats, and for them the moral defense of Western civilization and culture is not simply summed up in "Christ versus anti-Christ" slogans. Oronzo Reale, Secretary of the Republican Party, has observed: "Our Western citizenship . . . is not the acceptance of this or that political system, of this or that social system, but the acceptance of a civilization in which all choices are possible, against a civilization in which no choice is possible, given the rigidity of the system whch governs it." [49]

Communist moralism has already been evidenced with Pietro Ingrao's definition of politics as a struggle between "your world and ours." Ingrao's statement is not typical of Italian Communist thinking, however. He represents the very small group of Communists who personally suffered under Fascism, lived in exile, and fought in Spain and in the resistance movement in northern Italy between 1943 and 1945. The great mass of Communists are not Marxist ideologists; their education is too inadequate for them to understand Marxism. Even the leadership groups are now mainly Party and trade-union bureaucrats concerned primarily with maintaining their positions against competitors within the movement and holding onto their offices and perquisites. Many of these leaders suffered a great deal during the Fascist period and justify present relative opulence as a compensation for past sacrifices. The Italian Communist Party has not been a revolutionary party since the end of World War II.

The various sectors of Italian political life share an ingrained skepticism about human nature and a *Realpolitik* approach to international politics. They are the inheritors of a number of differing philosophical traditions, not necessarily indigenous to Italy. Common to all these traditions is the concept of the historical process as working toward certain goals that men can try to realize but cannot effectively oppose. Through Benedetto Croce, Italian liberalism was infected with German philosophical idealism. Catholic, Marxist, and Hegelian definitions of the ultimate directions and goals of history are not identical, but men of these persuasions find it easy to equate their preferences and hopes with the "wave of the future." Sometimes they assert the existence of a dominant trend in a particular historical period, and then rationalize behavior on this basis.

Prior to World War I, Italy had to participate in the partition of Africa, so the imperialists explained, because it was the trend of the times. In the Fascist outlook of Mussolini and Ciano, there was an inevitable trend toward war and the decadence of the democracies.[50] After World War II, the Italians saw an inevitable trend toward the end of European colonial empires as they watched and bitterly enjoyed the troubles of France and Britain in their overseas territories. Count Carlo Sforza, then Foreign Minister, assured the Chamber of Deputies in 1949 that Italy approved of independence for Libya and Eritrea because it was in the interest of Italy "not to go against the current." [51] Of course, the Italian Government had fought vigorously since 1945 to retain the colonies, and had discovered this new current only after losing the fight. The Communist opposition attacked Sforza for not taking this position three years earlier, and Sforza could reply only that the time then had not been politically ripe, that the Italian people had not been ready.[52]

Many backers of European federation have argued that it is the "law of the future." [53] The number of true federalists in Italy is small. Nevertheless, there is a traditional basis for a supranational political community. It need only be mentioned here that both the Catholic and Marxist traditions were, in the past, antinationalistic. The present status of Marxist internationalism is debatable. The old formulas of proletarian internationalism are still used freely, although the Communists, of course, oppose Western European unity as slavery to international monopoly capitalism.

Catholic attitudes have changed radically. The Church now supports the nationalist movements behind the Iron Curtain and in the Afro-Asian world as perhaps the only checks on Communist domination or expansion. Recently the Church has made a revision of its history of Italy. The occasion was a conference of Catholic scholars held in the summer of 1959 at the Catholic University of the Sacred Heart in Milan, with the theme "The Catholics and the Unity of Italy." Remarkably, it was concluded that the Catholic Church had not opposed national unity for Italy during the Risorgimento. Pius IX, it was decided, had opposed Italian nationalism only because Cavour was anticlerical, refused all accommodations with the Church, and advocated a "free Church in a free state." [54]

Despite this conclusion, it would be going too far to argue that Catholic universalism and internationalism no longer exist.

The radical republican tradition in Italy is also supranational. Mazzini was the founder of Young Italy, but he was also the founder of Young Europe. He loved his country because he loved all countries. For him, national unity and independence were only stepping-stones to a political community of the European continent.

These forces for European federalism suffer, of course, from their varied concepts of a federalized Europe. Guelphs and Ghibellines both favored universal empire but fought over the nature of the empire and the seat of power within it. Neo-Guelphs and neo-Ghibellines today may both preach that the age of the nation-state is ending, but their vision of the future commonwealth is little more than an enlargement of their immediate desires in domestic politics.

Something of the missionary tradition still remains. Catholic politicians still refer to the "universalism" of Italian thought, its "plurinational" sources of feeling and inspiration.[55] Fascist and non-Fascist appeals to the tradition of imperial Rome were motivated by civilizing-mission aspects as well as naked power drives. Non-Fascist, non-Catholic politicians are not immune to these attitudes. Liberals, Republicans, and other intellectuals consider themselves heirs of a tremendous, historic, millenary civilization; only with difficulty can they reconcile themselves to the vast gulf between Italy's present political status and its ancient glory. The most consistent policy, pursued by all postwar Italian governments, has been to make the Italian *presenza* felt on the international stage. There is usually a close relationship between the missionary complex and the inferiority complex. In Italian history, the assertion of a mission in international politics coincided with periods of dissension and weakness. The result was catastrophe for Italy and its neighbors.

II

Sources of Political
Power and Their
Impact on Foreign Policy

4

THE PARTY ORGANIZATIONS

THE CONSTITUTIONAL PARTIES

In Italy, control of the political parties lies with the cadre of full-time officials at the top of the party hierarchy, the executive bureau (*direzione*). In practically every party, the executive bureau is elected by the party central committee (sometimes called the national council), which is elected by the party congress. Nonetheless, the executive bureau usually manipulates the central committee and the party congress. It achieves this through the paid party secretaries of the regional, provincial, and local organizations, who are on the national party payroll and who control local section meetings and provincial congresses that elect the delegates to the party congress. Factionalism exists in all parties; in the Christian Democratic and Socialist parties, it is severe. Except for the Communist Party, the general practice is to have each faction represented on the executive bureau, unless it has abandoned the party completely. Consequently, policy issues are still fought out and decided at the top. The provincial and local party bureaucrats follow a factional leader and support a policy position, but they have little or no role in deciding that position. The party bureaucracies renew themselves by a process of co-optation or heredity. They control the candidacies to public office. The central committee can reject any candidate for the Chamber of Deputies or Senate who has been nominated by a regional or local party organization. It can punish an obstreperous deputy or senator by preventing his renomination or by shifting his candidacy from a district where he can win to one where he is certain to lose. Naturally, the factional leaders do some logrolling to get the most for their men, thus pre-

47

venting intraparty warfare. Parliamentarians are eligible for a pension if they serve more than six years, and elections are required at least every five years. The pension, while not munificent, is fairly generous by Italian standards, and so the parliamentarian is usually eager to get re-elected. But if he is to do so, he must not cause his leaders much trouble. This factor, among others, keeps the deputies and senators in line.

This system, known as the *partitocrazia*, has been bitterly denounced by some, notably Ignazio Silone and Giuseppe Maranini,[1] and defended by others. Giovanni Malagodi, the Secretary-General of the Liberal Party, defends it on the grounds that (1) politics in the middle of the twentieth century is a full-time job; (2) all aspects of life are becoming bureaucratized; (3) the old world of the local notables is dying. We live in a world of vast masses and nation-wide pressure groups, he argues, and the party organization mediates among these entrenched interests. It is the only organized group having some kind of vision of a national interest.[2]

The consequence of this system is to take away political power from the Cabinet and Parliament. Parliamentarians vote *en bloc* according to party. At the end of a debate in the Chamber or Senate, the party spokesman for the particular area of policy—foreign affairs, labor, agriculture, etc.—will announce how the members of his party will vote.* Discipline is imposed not by a caucus of parliamentarians, but by the party's executive bureau, which also includes nonparliamentarians and members of the other house. A breach of discipline is an event of prime importance, receiving extensive comment in the newspapers. The offending parliamentarian will, at the least, be brought before the central committee and denounced. The strongest punishment is expulsion from the party, which practically guarantees defeat at the next election. Independents do not win elections without party backing.

Cabinet crises result from decisions made by the party executive bureaus, not by votes in Parliament. Most dissolved Cabinets have

---

* After the debate on ratification of the European Common Market and Euratom, Senator Emilio Lussu of the left wing of the Socialist Party announced that the Socialist senators would abstain on the Common Market and vote for Euratom. He declared that he personally was voting this way only "for the sake of party discipline." Otherwise, he would have voted against both. Italy, Senato della Repubblica, *Atti parlamentari*, 2nd Leg., Vols. 1957, p. 24080.

fallen without a vote of no confidence in either house. Since 1945, the Christian Democratic Party has formed the core of all governments, and most of these went down (except when Parliament was dissolved for general elections) when the party's executive bureau decided on a reshuffling. On several occasions, the downfall came because a small allied party abandoned the coalition. In a few instances, the abandonment was not the real cause of the downfall; it served merely as the occasion for the Christian Democratic executive bureau to overturn the government.

Major policy issues are fought out in the party executive bureaus. Here the pressures are focused: The secretary-general and the vice-secretaries are the targets of the Church, business, agriculture, foreign governments, when they seek action by the Cabinet, Parliament, or ministerial bureaucracies. Sometimes, when quick action is required, the formal government is completely bypassed. This occurred in October, 1957, when a revolt broke out against the Communist-led government of the tiny Republic of San Marino. Amintore Fanfani, then Secretary-General of the Christian Democratic Party, personally directed the Italian action against San Marino from party headquarters in the Piazza del Gesu in Rome. At his command, all approaches to San Marino were blocked by Italian tanks, yet his only governmental position was as a member of the Chamber of Deputies.

The system is not as monolithic as it first appears. When the executive bureau agrees on policy, there is no question of its predominance over Parliament and the government. For example, Prime Minister Antonio Segni, on instructions from his party's executive bureau, submitted the resignation of his one-party Christian Democratic government in February, 1960. No vote of confidence was taken in Parliament. However, the system is not as absolute as an organizational chart might indicate. There is something of the anarchist in all men, and Italians will conform only so long before revolting. So the organization occasionally loses control. Central committees, and sometimes party congresses, force compromises on the *partitocrazia* and sometimes even smash them. A strong personality may upset the system. The much vaunted *partitocrazia* of the Socialist Party, which was presumably committed to continued close cooperation with the Communists (it is claimed that many Socialist Party bureaucrats were on the Communist payroll), has fought a losing battle against Pietro Nenni, and he has gradually succeeded in steering the party to a position of substantial independence on national and international questions without splitting the party wide open.

The Christian Democratic *partitocrazia* built up by Amintore Fanfani between 1954 and 1958 was temporarily wrecked in January, 1959, when he was overturned by internal enemies and high ecclesiasts. Of these three major parties, the Communist *partitocrazia* functions with the greatest efficiency, yet it has suffered factional infighting, defections of important leaders after the Hungarian uprising, and growing apathy of the rank and file and even of Party activists.

Strictly foreign-policy matters have never been the issue in internal party struggles. But the domestic issues involved often affect foreign policy. The principal issue in Italian foreign policy is whether to preserve or change the domestic social structure. This is, perhaps, the major thesis of this book, and will be elaborated upon at much greater length. One illustration may be useful here. The split in the Socialist Party in 1947, which led to the creation of what several years later became the Italian Social Democratic Party, was caused by a divergence of views on the relationship of the Socialists to the Italian Communist Party. This led, naturally, to a divergence of views on foreign policy. Yet it was basically a domestic question of domestic political power, concerning which other forces in Italian politics would be acceptable political allies.

This does not mean that party leaders have not had views, and disagreements, on foreign policy. It means only that they did not feel their convictions deeply enough to precipitate a serious crisis. The closest approach to a governmental crisis over foreign policy occurred in the period before 1949 when Alcide De Gasperi sought to lead his party to the fundamental decision to join the Western bloc and NATO. He himself had hesitated. But when he had been persuaded of the necessity by his Foreign Minister, Count Carlo Sforza, he found that a large section of his party leadership, especially the group around the left-wing Christian idealist Giuseppe Dossetti, was not convinced. (Dossetti has since left politics and entered the priesthood.) There was a neutralist tradition among many Christian Democrats and in certain Church circles. In the left wing of the party, the Atlantic alliance was identified as the foreign-policy counterpart of domestic social and economic conservatism. Finally, De Gasperi took Sforza to see Pope Pius XII, who also had misgivings. Sforza talked to the Pope. The opposition within the Christian Democratic Party ceased.

This story illustrates the special nature of the Christian Democratic Party organization. For a number of years after World War II ended, the party was more paper than real. The voters were rounded up by the civic committees of the Catholic Action Society, a lay organization under direct supervision of the bishop in each diocese. The party was a league of different interests—old notables, local satraps, Christian trade unionists, farm organizations, business-group spokesmen, Catholic intellectual associations, leaders of Catholic Action, etc. All were represented on the party's National Council and in its executive bureau. Only after Fanfani became Secretary-General was a real party organization built up. This organization did not absorb the others; it became one more among the rest, and Fanfani had to make alliances with some groups to check others. There were unstable coalitions, whose members demanded concrete concessions in return for problematic loyalty, and sought support from prominent churchmen in fighting against other factions backed by other prominent churchmen.

Fanfani's efforts to unite this party organizationally broke down in 1959, when his government was overthrown by internal opposition; it remains a league of widely contrasting interests today. An outside body, the Vatican, prevents it from flying apart and tries to mediate among the conflicting factions as an outside body. The Russian Communist Party may play a similar role among Italian Communist factions.

The split in the Sicilian Christian Democratic Party, engineered by Silvio Milazzo, has produced some surprises. Not only did the party lose control over Milazzo and his newly formed Sicilian Christian Social Union, but it apparently also lost control over the regular party organization in Sicily. There is some evidence that the Communist Party is also having trouble in keeping control over its Sicilian organization.[3]

Discipline in the Christian Democratic Party dropped to a low point in the spring of 1960, after the fall of the Segni Monocolore (one-party minority government), which had been supported by Monarchists and Fascists. The party executive bureau, by majority vote, authorized first Segni and later Fanfani to form a Center-Left coalition—Christian Democratic, Social Democratic, Republican, supported by the Socialists. A minority in the bureau and in the party's parliamentary delegation threatened to bolt and vote against such a government, thereby preventing realization of the much dis-cussed "opening to the left." With the Fascists' support, Fernando Tambroni finally formed a "purely administrative" Cabinet. This challenge to party discipline by the right-wing Christian Democrats (a challenge that left-wing Christian Democrats have never succeeded in making against many Center-Right governments) succeeded be-cause the rebels had the backing of high Church prelates. After the dust had settled, an authoritative editorial in L'Osservatore romano of May 17, 1960, stated that the problem of collaboration with parties "who do not admit religious principles" must always be decided by ecclesiastical authorities and never by the individual faithful.[4] The Vatican could not enforce this policy, however, and in February, 1962, a new alliance was constructed, with Socialist support.

The Christian Democratic Party is made up of a loose coalition of interest groups and, as a consequence, lacks a broad party concept of foreign affairs. Most party leaders concern themselves with foreign issues only when these impinge directly on their immediate con-stituents. The voting support of the party comes from largely apo-litical sectors of the population: women, the aged, small peasant proprietors with specific, limited interests;[5] thus, the top leaders have little within the party to restrain them in many broad areas of foreign affairs. The restraints come from outside the party—from the Church or from other countries.

Most of the smaller constitutional parties (i.e., their stated aims are nonrevolutionary) are under tight organizational control. The Liberal Party is completely under the thumb of its Secretary-General, Giovanni Malagodi, who has converted it into a simple spokesman of the Confederation of Industrialists (Confindustria). It is the most orthodox of all parties in its classical market economics and its pro-Western orientation. Its left wing, New Dealish in tendency, abandoned the party in 1953 to form the minuscule Radical Party (in the French meaning of the word), because of domestic issues, particularly the total subservience to big business. The Liberals have more influence on foreign policy than their limited voting strength would indicate. As the party of conservative respectability, uncontaminated with even a left wing, such as is present among the Christian Democrats, it attracts support from professional men and upper-level government bureaucrats. These include numerous Foreign Office bureaucrats, who maintain regular contacts with Liberal Party leaders. Relations are close with the right wing of the Christian Democrats, the faction headed by Giuseppe Pella. Except for the Fanfani interlude in the last half of 1958, Liberals or conservative Christian Democrats, and their allies in the Foreign Office bureaucracy, have dominated the Foreign Ministry since the days of Alcide De Gasperi.

The Social Democratic Party has lost the wing that gave priority to the achievement of Socialist unity, and the remnants of the party are dominated by its Secretary-General, Giuseppe Saragat. The party is so much the emanation of this one man that serious doubt exists as to whether the party could survive his demise. The executive bureau is completely in his hand. He can abolish the party newspaper, *Giustizia*, one week and reinstate it the next. One week he can be for disengagement in Central Europe and the next week against it.

The Republican Party is split into two factions, the majority faction led by Ugo La Malfa, and the minority by Randolfo Pacciardi. The difference is not over foreign policy; both groups support Italian membership in the Western alliance. La Malfa advocated the "opening to the left," while Pacciardi opposed it. In effect, the question was whether the Socialist Party was to be brought into the support of a Center-Left government with the domestic consequences that would follow. It was generally agreed among both Italians and non-Italians that no foreign-policy changes of consequence would ensue.[6]

The "Revolutionary" Opposition

The Neo-Fascist Party (Italian Social Movement) and Monarchist (Italian Democratic) Party are usually identified as the parties of the right-wing revolutionary opposition. Today this classification is purely theoretical, since it is based on party goals that are incompatible with a constitutional republic. There is little constitutionalism in Italy, as indicated earlier in the discussion of the relation of the party executive bureaus to Parliament. The Fascists are not anti-republican; most of their leaders draw their inspiration from Mussolini's Fascist Social Republic, instituted in October, 1943, behind the German lines in northern Italy. There is no point in the adjective "Neo," and the fascists themselves do not use it. They are not new but old, the relics of a not-forgotten past. The Monarchists have even dropped the symbol of the monarchy. The focus of their loyalty is less Umberto of Savoy, the King in exile, than Achille Lauro, ex-Mayor of Naples and a wealthy shipping magnate. He has largely converted the party into an instrument of southern revendication, and conservative, if not reactionary, defense of entrenched interests.[7] Devoted believers in the monarchical principle are a minority in the party today. Since 1958, the Monarchists have been in a steady decline.

In one sense, there is a basis for calling them parties of "unconstitutional" opposition. Much of their electoral strength has come from "protest" voters, as is also the case with the Socialists and Communists. The Fascist protesters are a queer combination of the economically disinherited, those who collaborated with the Nazis after 1943, and those suffused with nostalgia for the old days of bombast and pseudoglory. Rome is the most Fascist city in Italy. It is full of bureaucrats and retired pensioners originally brought to the capital when Mussolini was buying support by expanding the government machine and padding the public payroll. In the 1958 general election, Rome elected four of the twenty-four Fascist deputies and one of the eight Fascist senators. The Fascist Party was a member of the governing coalition that controlled the City Council until 1961. Filippo Anfuso, a Fascist senator today, was *chef de cabinet* in the later years of Ciano's tenure at the Foreign Ministry and stayed with Mussolini to the end in 1945.[8] He can walk in and visit old friends at the Foreign Office any time.

A good part of the Monarchist vote has come from the southern subproletariat, as a protest against degrading conditions and in response to sectional appeals and vote buying. The post-1958 decline of the Monarchists has occurred mainly because of desertions by this sector of its electorate, which has come to realize that the Fascist and Monarchist leadership has been well domesticated. Since the middle 1950's, the leaders of these parties have manipulated their parliamentary delegations and local councilors to support the right wing of Christian Democracy. Both proclaim themselves Catholic parties, committed to the 1929 Lateran agreements and Mussolini's "reconciliation" between Church and State. From 1956 to 1960, separately or together, they provided the parliamentary votes that enabled Christian Democratic governments to stay in power—with one exception: Fanfani's Christian Democratic–Social Democratic coalition from July, 1958, to January, 1959. Even earlier, they provided the votes in many city councils, such as Rome's, that enabled Christian Democrats to lead coalitions that controlled local governments, especially in the south. Since political parties are not charitable organizations, a price must be paid for these services—a fair share of the rewards from *sottogoverno*, the graft, favors, and patronage.

Fascists and Monarchists have caused little or no trouble in foreign policy, except to give a nationalistic tone to certain Italian pronouncements on issues such as Trieste and the South Tirol. But they are not alone on these issues. They are nostalgic about the "glorious" days of the 1930's, when Italy's "voice" shook the world. They are contemptuous of the French, hate the British, and disdain American liberalism and equalitarianism. They are firm believers in hierarchy and a socially structured society. But they have voted down the line, since the days of their domestication, for Western or Atlantic orientation, regarding it as a basic foreign-policy plank that supports their domestic position. Except for a few extreme Fascists, they are not a radical Right but rather a conservative or reactionary Right. The Suez crisis of 1956 gave them, as well as others, a field day, enabling them to vent their spleen against Britain and France, safe in the coinciding of their emotions with United States and United Nations policy.

THE LEFT OPPOSITION

The Italian Socialist Party and the Italian Communist Party made up the Left opposition until 1962. The Socialist Party, formally founded in 1892, is the oldest organized party still functioning. The Liberals and Republicans have still older traditions, going back to Cavour and Mazzini respectively, but these traditions are different from party organizations. The Socialist Party suffered numerous schisms before and after World War I and after World War II. It has had a "maximalist" revolutionary tradition, which has survived the break-off of moderate revisionist elements on its right and extremist Communist elements on its left.[9] Its revolutionary maximalism, however, has usually been more verbal than effectual, and by 1960 there was little evidence of militancy associated with vibrant challenges to the constituted order. In effect, it had become domesticated and "reformist," a dirty word in the true revolutionist's lexicon.

The party's foreign-policy tradition is antimilitaristic and neutralistic, conforming to the pre-World War I orientation of the Second International. The Socialist Party opposed joining the Triple Alliance before 1915 and opposed Italy's entry into the war on the side of the Triple Entente. It was anti-imperialistic and opposed Giolitti's Libyan expedition in 1911–12. However, it has had very little interest in foreign policy. Its preoccupation then and to a great extent now is with the revendication of the claims of the workers, especially in the north. Foreign-policy attitudes reflected the impact of external events on the achievement of these claims, and the chances of success for the party.

The Socialist Party is the third largest in Italy. It has long since ceased to be the sole representative of the working masses; the Communists and Christian Democrats each draw greater support from this sector of the population. Unlike the other two, it was unable to survive the Fascist rule, having neither the conspiratorial effectiveness of the Communists nor the protection of the Vatican.

During the Fascist period, the party leadership, exiled in France, entered into a unity-of-action agreement with the Communists. This was temporarily dissolved in 1939, at the time of the Soviet-Nazi nonaggression pact, but restored after 1941. Pietro Nenni, who led the party then as now, took the position then and after World War II that when Socialists fight Communists, reaction triumphs. He attributed the original victories of Fascism and Nazism to disunity among the proletarian parties.[10]

The Communist Party emerged after 1946 as the larger of the two proletarian parties and the dominant element in the labor confederation, and this, combined with Nenni's conciliatory attitude, led to Socialist subservience to Communist tactics. In 1947, a right-wing faction split off from the Socialist Party over this situation to carry a minority of the Socialist deputies and voters into what finally became the Italian Social Democratic Party. In 1948, the Socialists and Communists ran a joint ticket in the general election. This was the high point of their collaboration.

In foreign policy, the party opposed Italy's entry into NATO in 1949, falling back upon the traditional neutralist arguments. Since that time, collaboration with the Communists has gradually declined at the national level, although it continues in the trade-union movement, cooperatives, and numerous local governments. The unity-of-action pact was terminated in 1952. Since 1953, separate tickets have been nominated in all elections. Relations between the two parties were becoming increasingly strained even before the Polish and Hungarian revolts of 1956, and these two events strengthened the Socialist factions, now led by Nenni himself, who wanted complete autonomy for the party.

By 1957, Communists and Socialists had split on foreign policy. The Communists opposed Italy's entry into both Euratom and the Common Market; the Socialists favored Euratom and abstained on the Common Market, but did not totally oppose it. One of their leading spokesmen, Riccardo Lombardi, recognized that the Common Market had good aspects, such as the stimulus it would give to modernizing Italy's productive apparatus. He criticized the Communists for protecting outmoded and inefficient facilities under the guise of protecting the workers' jobs.[11] The Socialists objected to the business-cartel characteristics of the Common Market, but saw the possibility of offsetting these with a labor cartel. The party also saw in the Common Market a chance to broaden Italian labor contacts with the Western labor movement.

By 1958, Nenni was openly stating that the Socialists no longer objected to Italy's membership in NATO, especially as the emphasis on economic collaboration and mutual aid was now superseding the military aspects. In the spring of 1960, the Socialists collaborated with the Social Democrats, Republicans, and the majority of the

Christian Democratic executive bureau in an effort to form a Center-Left government. It failed, because of the behavior of the right-wing Christian Democrats, as has already been mentioned. In 1962, however, it appears to have succeeded.

During these long years of gradual realignment of Socialist orientation, the party has been fairly effective in maintaining discipline and control. Largely because of Nenni's caution and gradualness, no splits have occurred since the 1947 schism that produced the Social Democratic Party. The Socialists have recouped their losses, partially at the expense of the Social Democrats. As late as 1959, five Social Democratic deputies went over to the Socialist group in Parliament. Nenni's big problem has been the threat of a schism on his left, involving the faction known as the *Carristi,* which is still enamored of the myth of proletarian unity.

During its years as an opposition party, when many of the Center-Right forces regarded it as beyond the pale of political respectability, the Socialist Party had negligible influence on foreign policy. Socialists had no contacts, not even any sources of information, in the Foreign Office bureaucracy. In this respect, the Communists were more successful. Whatever minimal influence the Socialists exerted was through President Gronchi, whose election in 1955 was maneuvered by Nenni.

The Socialist influence has been exerted in favor of *détente* and disengagement. The Socialists believe that such policies would more than promote peace and survival; they would also contribute to the forces moderating the totalitarian characteristics of the Soviet system. The Socialists tend to consider the centralization, bureaucratization, intensive internal discipline, and emphasis on heavy industry that prevail in the Soviet system as products of the insecurities of international life rather than as inevitable features of a Socialist society. The Socialists feel that the unity of the Soviet bloc reflects a high level of international tension, obeying the same psychological motivations that operate among states of the Western world.

The Socialists consider intensive Cold War as the best external circumstance for maintaining the Right in power inside Italy. The polarization of international politics can cause the polarization of internal politics. The opening to the left appeared more possible in an international atmosphere of *détente,* and it is not surprising that this domestic consequence of international politics has dominated Socialist thinking.

The Italian Communist Party is the largest Communist Party in the Western world in terms of membership and the second-largest party in Italy in terms of votes. The membership claimed for 1959 was 1,789,269, down from the peak of 2,242,719 claimed for 1949.[12] (These are Communist figures and probably exaggerated.) In the 1958 general election, the Party received 6,704,454 votes for its candidates to the Chamber of Deputies, 22.7 per cent of the votes cast, and elected 140 deputies.[13] The dominant leadership of Palmiro Togliatti, Secretary-General, and Luigi Longo, Vice Secretary-General, has effectively controlled the Party's executive bureau, secretariat, and central committee throughout the postwar period. Dissidents have been isolated or sloughed off, and numerical losses have been minimized. The challengers have been beaten down with the usual slogans of "dogmatism" and "revisionism." Loyalty to the Soviet Union has been maintained, in the face of some internal opposition and despite all the vicissitudes of Soviet domestic and international life—the Titoist heresy, the downgrading of Stalin and the Stalinists, the Polish and Hungarian uprisings. In Togliatti's words,

> . . . the tie with the Soviet Union has been our life, it has been the essential part of the life and of the conscience of the working class and of its vanguard; therefore, this tie is put above and beyond the debate which we all want to conduct and which has always been conducted, on the way to resolve determinate problems, on the criticisms which must or must not be made.[14]

At the same time, the Party has affirmed the right to "the full and autonomous responsibility of each [Communist] Party for its own activity." [15]

In the postwar period, the Italian Communists have faithfully followed the Soviet line on foreign policy. They opposed the Marshall Plan, NATO, the European Defense Community, the Common Market, Euratom, etc. They vigorously supported the propaganda campaign of the "Partisans of Peace"; they warmed up to Nasser when Soviet-Egyptian relations were warm and cooled off when Soviet-Egyptian relations were strained. Their formal prescription for Italian foreign policy, reaffirmed at the Ninth Party Congress, in Rome in February, 1960, is a position equidistant between the Eastern and Western blocs.[16] But this prescription is for a non-Communist Italy; a Communist Italy would probably immediately enter the Soviet bloc, although the Italian Communists do not say so explicitly. (One speculation is that for tactical reasons a Communist-controlled Italy might not openly and immediately join the Warsaw Pact grouping.)

The Communists' unsuccessful opposition to all the major choices made by the Italian Government since 1947, when the Communists and Socialists were forced out of the government, suggests that Italian Communism has absolutely no influence on foreign-policy decisions. This overstates the case, for a host of minor choices—especially economic—and the tone and presentation of government policies are affected by the Communist Party's presence. ,

The Communist Party has deep roots in Italian society; it is not a marginal group, isolated from social, civic, and personal contact with the broad life of the nation. Its organizations extend everywhere, and so do its personal contacts. A Party section exists in almost every village and in every quarter in the towns and cities. No other political party has such a network—not even the Christian Democrats, who must rely on the church parish organizations in many localities. In fact, only the network of Catholic parishes approaches the Communist one, and there are remote hamlets where a Communist Party organization exists but not a parish church. The number of party cells, announced at the Ninth Party Congress, was 39,852, down from the 56,044 claimed in 1956 at the Eighth Party Congress.[17] It is still an impressive figure. The number of sections was 11,097, down from 11,262 in 1956, but still sufficient for maintaining grass-roots contacts, performing the whole gamut of services characteristic of American political machines.

The Party's masses come from the industrial workers, landless farm laborers, and sharecroppers,[18] but its leaders come from all levels of Italian society. They have relatives and friends in the upper strata of the state bureaucracy, in big business, in the cultural and educational world, in the Church and the Vatican, in the armed forces. Many of them come from the "right" families and have entrée to practically any social group because family connections count. They went to school and to the university with the leaders of the dominant political and nonpolitical groups of Italian life. I am almost tempted to say that in Italy there also is an "establishment." Thus, the Communists are not strange, invisible, terrible devils to the Italian people. Almost every Italian knows at least one Communist.

Communists cooperated in the resistance movement in World War II, and they were members of the Committee of National Liberation coalition governments from 1944 until 1947. In the Senate and Chamber of Deputies, the Communists are the second-largest bloc on the floor and, in consequence, have the second-largest representation on the various substantive committees. Communist floor leaders are in constant communication with the leaders of the other parties, to operate the machinery of Parliament, to plan the agenda, to schedule the debates. Communist senators and deputies lunch with other members of Parliament, meet them in the lounges and bars, libraries and barbershops, of the Chamber and Senate buildings. These contacts, though they may lack the intimacy reserved for fellow Party members, are nonetheless human relationships. A Christian Democratic senator may take the floor to denounce Communism as the essence of the anti-Christ, and later meet a fellow-senator Communist in the bar to tell him not to take his attack too seriously. A Communist deputy who gets seriously ill will probably receive as many cards from Christian Democratic and other politicians as he will from fellow Party members.

Businessmen find that making economic contacts with Soviet-bloc states is facilitated by using the Italian Party as an intermediary. The low living standards of many workers and, in the past, mass unemployment have supported the Communist argument that Italy cannot afford to ignore any possible market by indulging in ideological prejudice. In 1948, De Gasperi sent a trade mission to Moscow to negotiate an agreement on nonstrategic items. The purpose was to gain trade and provide work, and also to take away some of the thunder of the opposition's claim that Italy's entry into the Atlantic political and economic system would cost Italy a heavy economic price.[19] Thus, the Left opposition can influence Italian foreign policy by forcing the government to meet some of its demands. The Communist Party in

Italy is large enough and powerful enough so that the vast noncommitted majority continue to support it as a form of insurance in the event of its coming to power.[20]

Between 1944 and 1947, the Italian Communist Party was part of the government. Communist politicians were appointed ambassadors to some Eastern European states, and there was a tendency to clear government policy toward the Soviet-area states with the Italian Communist Party.[21] This ended in 1947, but the Communists can still affect Italian policy by the image they present as local spokesmen for the Soviet Union. The non-Communists assume that the policy of the Italian Party is invariably the policy line of the Soviet Government. Since the Soviets cannot be ignored, the Italian Government reacts, one way or the other, to the Italian Communist stand on an issue. Thus, the Italian Communists, by taking a stand on an issue, force the government to choose the other side, to demonstrate its anti-Communism to the United States or to the Church, and to appear to be unyielding in its opposition so that the latter cannot claim a victory. The government can also use Italian Communism for its own purposes. In September, 1947, De Gasperi sent a message to Tarchiani, his Ambassador in Washington, directing him to use the threat of Communism to get more American aid, warning that if it was not forthcoming, it might be necessary to bring Nenni and Togliatti back into the Cabinet.[22]

But although the Italian Communists adopt the Soviet position on basic issues, they do not always merely follow. For example, the Italian Communists' opposition to establishing United States medium-range-missile bases in Italy in 1958 led to the proposal that renunciation of these bases be traded for Soviet renunciation of missile bases in Albania. This proposal appears to have originated in Italy, not in Moscow. After it was offered publicly, the Italian Communists had to send a delegation to Moscow to persuade Soviet leaders to adopt it. Moscow was persuaded, but the Italian and American governments were not.

The Italian Communists affect Italian foreign policy most through their domestic operations. The major goal of Italian foreign policy is to preserve the domestic social structure and resist major social reform; the Communists, by their participation in Italian political life, have contributed to the successful pursuit of this goal. Despite the extremist, revolutionary nature of the Communists' ideology, their efforts for agrarian and industrial reform have been mainly verbal. They have frozen a large bloc of votes and potentially effective groups, such as the Italian General Confederation of Labor (CGIL), into sterile, often reactionary positions: they have made it extremely difficult for the Socialists to break out of the same trap for fear of being attacked as enemies of the working class, their base of support. In this way, the Communists paved the way for some of the victories of the Right. They are content to dominate the opposition, since they are not strong enough to assume power. As a result, they were a major cause of Italy's past political immobility. The Italian Communists—and they are not unique in this— have always put power ahead of the people's welfare. It should not be surprising if they use foreign policy as well as domestic policy to achieve this power.

5

THE PARLIAMENT, THE CABINET, AND THE PRESIDENT

THE PARLIAMENT

The Italian Parliament, like the government of which it is a part, has little prestige. The basic fact is that the party bureaucracies, not the legislators, run the Parliament. Before a vote of confidence is ever taken in Parliament, the government's fate has been determined by the party executive bureaus. Thus the Parliament is "an organ without a voice at the crucial moments of Italian life." [1]

The reasons given for the parliamentarians' subservience are many and difficult to weigh: modern mass society and the bureaucratization of life, a culture that emphasizes servility and conformity, a system of proportional representation that makes party backing essential for election to Parliament.

The position of senator or deputy has strong attractions, both honorific and economic. The title "Honorable" is acquired with the seat but is not lost when the seat is lost; it can be engraved on calling cards forever after. This is a major inducement, as the hunt for titles is more vigorous now, under the republic, than it was under the monarchy. Also, a seat in Parliament pays relatively well. It is a better-paying job than working for the party press, the party secretariat, or a party-related trade-union organization; only business spokesmen do better. After serving six years in Parliament, a member is entitled to a life pension of respectable size, as Italian pensions go. But elections are held every *five* years, or less, so that a member must be re-elected at least once to get the pension. Members of the Parliament are, therefore, desperately eager to be re-elected, and this economic stake, among others, makes them captives of the party leadership.

A hostile critic has divided the present generation of parliamentarians into four groups:

1. Ministers or potential ministers: members for whom getting into or staying in the Cabinet is everything. Every question is resolved according to the anticipated effect on the individual's career.

2. The "court": other members of Parliament whose fortunes are tied to the fortunes of a potential minister.

3. The organization men: members of the *apparat* of the party, or the union, or a pressure group. Their personal influence depends on their organization's power, which will draw a group of clients to them. They want to develop their organization and their position in it.

4. The others: members without any particular abilities, who must please their superiors in order to get renominated. But they try not to get identified with a particular current within the party so as to avoid sharing any possible failures.[2]

This breakdown is somewhat arbitrary. Obviously, it does not apply to most of the small parties, although even these have factionalism. Of the three large parties—Christian Democratic, Socialist, and Communist—it does not apply to the Communists, where factionalism also exists. It applies in part to the Socialists, although they have been out of the government for so long that Cabinet fever has not been a potent influence on behavior. It most accurately applies to the Christian Democrats.

Policy decisions are made at party headquarters, not in Parliamentary caucuses. However, the leading members of Parliament are the leading party spokesmen. The Senate and Chamber of Deputies are equal in legal power, but the Chamber has greater political influence and the important party leaders are found here. Many foreign-policy decisions, even important ones, are not sufficiently interesting for party leaders to take them away from the Foreign Minister, who is usually a leader himself. This disinterest is echoed by a general disinterest in foreign policy among most parliamentarians. Absenteeism soars during foreign-policy debates, even on major issues, and there may be only thirty or forty out of six hundred deputies on the Chamber floor. In 1957, during the debate preceding ratification of the treaties creating the European Common Market and Euratom, attendance of both deputies and senators was very poor.[3]

On the rare occasions of open breakdown of party discipline, domestic issues have been involved. Fanfani was undermined in the winter of 1958–59 by *francs-tireurs* within his own party. But there is no record of discipline being broken in any party over foreign policy. An explanation for this was given to me by a deputy who is very active in foreign-policy issues and is a spokesman for his party on these issues in Parliament. "A deputy knows that he will not gain or lose a single vote by a position taken on foreign policy. He has no inducement to challenge the party leaders and every inducement not to." The indifference of the politicians reflects the indifference of the populace.

Individual members of Parliament may influence foreign policy because of their personal attributes. Former ministers and former undersecretaries have acquired both connections and experience that may make them useful and influential. For example, Vittorio Badini Confalonieri became an expert on the Common Market while Undersecretary of Foreign Affairs. He has been consulted constantly by Foreign Office bureaucrats and by subsequent ministers, even after he officially became just another deputy in the Chamber. Giorgio La Pira, Mayor of Florence, and a deputy from the Florentine constituency, has many connections in the Arab world. He acts as guide when visiting Arabian dignitaries come to see the sights of Rome and Florence. His connection with Fanfani and the Christian Democratic left wing has influenced their attitude toward the Middle East and North Africa. He is important to the Christian Democrats because he can give speeches at party congresses that help the party appear to be a left-wing party.

The Italian Parliament uses the system of substantive committees. Both Chamber and Senate have foreign-affairs committees. All committee work is done in executive session, although committee reports will be published and rumors and stories are always circulated. There is general agreement that these committees have no real power. The foreign embassies do not even bother to cultivate their chairmen. The standard explanation is that it is impossible to have a real and critical analysis of, say, foreign affairs within a committee whose second-largest component group is composed of Communists, for they would inform the Soviet Union of everything. The explanation is good as far as it goes. But the basic fact is that the foreign-affairs committees are not important because Parliament is not important.

THE CABINET

One political commentator defined the essential function of the Cabinet minister as mediating between two powers, the party apparatus, and the higher state bureaucracy.[4] The essential burden is on the individual minister, for the Cabinet does not appear to operate very effectively as a collective decision-making body. The individual minister benefits by not getting mixed up in other people's business. Also, it justifies him in keeping the others out of his matters.

Only high-level issues are brought before the Cabinet. For foreign-affairs questions, they are very high level indeed. Although what goes on at Cabinet meetings can never be told officially, it appears that when the Minister of Foreign Affairs discusses foreign policy inside the Cabinet, his purpose is to keep fellow Cabinet members *au courant*.

This situation may be modified by a number of factors: the political position of the Foreign Minister vis-à-vis fellow party members, the ambitions or skills of other ministers, the party composition of the Cabinet (one-party or coalition), the nature of the issue. There is only one standing committee of ministers on foreign affairs, the Interministerial Committee on the Common Market. When international issues cross departmental lines, temporary committees or informal consultations are organized among the ministers directly concerned. There is a permanent Supreme Defense Council; unlike the U.S. National Security Council, the Italian organization is limited to narrow military questions, and the foreign minister is not even a member. The Supreme Defense Council includes the President of Italy, the Prime Minister, the Defense Minister, and the Chief of Staff. Other ministers may be called in at times. It does not appear to be an important body, or one in which foreign-policy questions are regularly discussed.

Although the Christian Democratic Party has dominated postwar Italian Cabinets, especially since the Socialists and Communists were ejected from the Cabinet in 1947, coalition governments were the rule until the late 1950's. Then the possibility of heading the Foreign Ministry after a subsequent Cabinet reshuffling might induce a minor-party minister to discuss foreign policy in preparation for a future claim to the post and to demonstrate his party's concern about global matters. Former Foreign Ministers now holding other ministries might enter the discussion on the basis of previously acquired expertise. Former Undersecretaries of Foreign Affairs, in anticipation of subsequently becoming ministers, might debate foreign policy with the same justification.

After one-party Christian Democratic governments became more common, the possibility of Cabinet discussion and disagreement did not end. These governments had to satisfy various party factions in allocating Cabinet posts, and a factional leader holding another post might easily wrangle with the Foreign Minister over a question in the latter's sphere of competence. For example, indiscretions that broke into the Italian press in early 1958 revealed sharp attacks by Minister Without Portfolio Dino Del Bo, a left-wing Christian Democrat, against Foreign Minister Giuseppe Pella, a right-wing Christian Democrat.[5]

The crucial question involves the political power and authority of the Foreign Minister. The position does not carry the status and prestige of the United States Secretary of State or the British Foreign Minister. It is not recognized as the number-two post in the government. To be powerful, a Foreign Minister must depend on his personal authority. Count Carlo Sforza was Foreign Minister from 1947 to 1951, when illness forced him to retire. His personal authority derived from his past record as an anti-Fascist (still worth something in the late 1940's), his professional competence as a former career diplomat, and his connections in the Western world. However, he was the nominee of the Republican Party, the smallest and weakest of the four parties constituting the coalition. His personal authority would not have enabled him to carry out his foreign policy, but behind him was the power of Alcide De Gasperi, Prime Minister and leader of the Christian Democratic Party.

The influence wielded by the Foreign Minister depends also on the particular issue involved. If it directly affects an important outside group, the Church, or a large firm, this outside interest will go to the minister who can get it what it wants. These groups have access to all ministers, but are more influential with some than with others. Large business firms, for example, usually approach the ministers responsible for economic matters—industry, finance, treasury—and when these firms exert influence, these ministers act. If necessary, they will go to the party executive bureau to get a favorable decision.

The Prime Minister's role in foreign policy depends largely on the man, his political position, and his interests. A career officer of the Foreign Ministry is always assigned to the Prime Minister's office as liaison. Similar officers are also assigned to the Minister of Foreign Trade, the President, and the Secretary-General of the Christian Democratic Party. A weak Prime Minister, such as Antonio Segni or Adone Zoli, may hesitate to interfere with a Foreign Minister more politically powerful than himself. Zoli was fundamentally uninterested in foreign affairs and was quite willing to let his Foreign Minister, Giuseppe Pella, handle them alone. Only when a domestic political reaction occurred, giving ammunition to the opposition, would Zoli become involved.

Alcide De Gasperi was neither weak nor indifferent. From 1946 to 1953, he was Prime Minister uninterruptedly and undisputed leader of the Christian Democratic Party. In 1951, when Sforza retired, De Gasperi took on the Foreign Ministry in addition. From 1946 to 1951, not a single foreign-policy problem of any importance was decided without the joint collaboration of De Gasperi and the Foreign Minister and, if De Gasperi thought it necessary, the remaining members of the Council of Ministers. A special section within his personal office was set up to maintain relations with the Foreign Office. He was briefed daily on foreign affairs and tried to see visiting foreign politicians, newspapermen, and other dignitaries.[6] Sforza always sent the most important passages from his dispatches to De Gasperi.[7]

Since De Gasperi (he died in 1954, one year after the fall of his eighth government), no Christian Democratic politician has been able to exercise such authority. Fanfani, simultaneously Prime Minister, Foreign Minister, and Secretary-General of the party, came closest, but was still far from it, in his brief ministry, from July, 1958, to January, 1959. A weak Prime Minister permits the Cabinet ministers to follow independent, if not conflicting, policies. In the past decade, some ministers have pursued policies contrary to the Foreign Minister's, and the Foreign Minister, under conflicting pressures, may adopt inconsistent policies. In the spring of 1958, the Italian Government, under French pressure, refused to sell arms to Tunisia, but within two weeks invited President Nasser, who was sending arms to Tunisian nationalists, to make a formal visit to Rome.

In the spring of 1958, Defense Minister P. E. Taviani, who had had a term as an Undersecretary for Foreign Affairs, concluded agreements with the French and German governments on establishing joint arms-production facilities. He then presented the Foreign Office with a *fait accompli*. Because it fell within the broad policy of European integration, which was official Italian policy, Taviani's action could not be regarded as a double policy but rather as a difference of degree. He was ready to move faster than the Foreign Minister; he had not undercut the Foreign Minister.

The growing trend for national leaders outside the Foreign Office to conduct international negotiations has multiplied the possibilities for independent policies. When Ministers of agriculture, defense, finance, etc., lead delegations at international conferences, the Foreign Minister's control over policy is inevitably undermined, even if he is represented by subordinates. Even in conferences considered technical, political policies can be undermined.

Historically, the Undersecretary for Foreign Affairs has been of little importance in Italy.[8] Under Mussolini, who made a practice of simultaneously heading a number of ministries, including the Foreign Ministry, the Undersecretary became more of an operating chief. Dino Grandi, who became an Undersecretary in 1925, was quite malleable in the hands of the Foreign Office professionals.[9] Ciano, who took over the Palazzo Chigi in 1936, preferred to give no authority to the Undersecretary.

The number of Undersecretaries in the Foreign Ministry is not fixed by law. They are invariably parliamentarians and potential ministers. In recent years, there have been two Undersecretaries for Foreign Affairs; one confines himself to emigration questions, and the other serves as General Undersecretary. The latter may be given little or much to do, depending on the personality of his superior and their political relations. In a coalition government, the Undersecretary is often from a different party than the Foreign Minister. He tries to take on as much responsibility as possible—for his own and his party's benefit. In a one-party, Christian Democratic government, the Undersecretary is sometimes from a different faction. While Alberto Folchi, a follower of President Gronchi and of the party's left wing, was General Undersecretary, the Foreign Minister was either a right-wing Christian Democrat or a Liberal. Usually, Folchi was bypassed on issues concerning which he was in disagreement with the Foreign Minister.*

THE PRESIDENT

The Italian Chief of State has never had a purely honorific or formal role to play. The *Statuto albertino* of 1848, which became the Constitution of first the Kingdom of Sardinia and later the United Kingdom of Italy, stated that the government would be responsible. It failed to state to whom the government would be responsible. To the King, was the original assumption, but practice made the government responsible to a parliamentary majority. Nevertheless, the King remained an important influence on policy. The upper house, the Senate, was filled by royal appointment. A "court party" continued right into the beginning of the twentieth century. The King remained especially active in foreign and military policy. Often he personally chose the Foreign Minister and armed-services ministers (usually professional officers), and the ambassadors to the principal powers. He carried on an independent correspondence with key and personally close envoys, and occasionally issued instructions that might fail to coincide in all respects with the position of the responsible ministers.[10]

Under Mussolini, the major role of King Victor Emmanuel III in foreign policy declined—not that he opposed becoming Emperor of Ethiopia or King of Albania. The King signed the declaration of

* In the spring of 1958, Gronchi and Folchi wanted to sell arms to Tunisia, but were overruled by Foreign Minister Pella and the senior professionals in the Foreign Office who had acceded to French objections. Shortly after, Britain and the United States decided to sell arms to Tunisia. Pella was out of town when the British and American Ambassadors formally notified Italy of the Anglo-American decision. On instructions from the Secretary-General of the Foreign Office, they ignored Folchi, second in rank, and called instead on the Director-General of Political Affairs, Massimo Magistrati.

war on June 10, 1940, and there is no evidence that he disagreed with Mussolini's evaluation that Germany had won the war.

The Constitution of the Italian Republic set up a parliamentary form of government, with a President as Head of the State. His powers and functions are defined in Chapter II, Articles 83–91, of the Constitution. Of these, the most important, for our purposes, is to promulgate laws and issue decrees having the force of law. He also commands the armed forces, presides over the Supreme Defense Council, and, upon authorization of Parliament, declares war. Article 89 restricts the independent exercise of his powers, however, stating that no act of the president is legal unless it is countersigned by the responsible minister. All measures having the "value of law" must also be countersigned by the Prime Minister.[11]

The President's power, viewed legally, is primarily negative. He can refuse to sign a bill or decree. Parliament can override his refusal by repassing the bill with a simple majority. However, the Constitution says nothing about what the Cabinet can do if the President refuses to issue a decree.

The Italian Republic is too young and its institutions too immature to make it possible to settle many questions by precedent, and vigorous debates rage over the proper role of the head of state. The tradition inherited from the monarchy does not dictate a passive figurehead. To a considerable degree, the man can make the office.

The President has greater security in office than any other political leader. His salary and term of office, seven years, are fixed and not subject to votes of confidence. Once elected by a joint session of Parliament, he need not fear what it can do to him unless he has ambitions for re-election. He can be impeached on only two charges: high treason and attempted overthrow of the Constitution. Outside these, he cannot be held responsible for his acts in the exercise of his duties.

In its brief history, the Italian Republic has had one provisional President, Enrico De Nicola, 1946–48, and two Presidents, Luigi Einaudi, 1948–55, and Giovanni Gronchi, 1955–62. All three were men of strong opinions, and did not hesitate to express them. The first two, however, had an even stronger man to contend with, Prime Minister Alcide De Gasperi, who usually succeeded in dominating a situation. No commanding figure rose to succeed De Gasperi, and in the political free-for-all that followed, the Christian Democratic Party leadership was torn by confusion and contradiction. Meanwhile, President Einaudi was quietly sending back bills and executive decrees to be modified to meet his objections. In 1954, he insisted to the Prime Minister that he must nominate a Foreign Minister who would accept and sign the Trieste agreements. Gaetano Martino met his condition.

Giovanni Gronchi differed from Einaudi less in activity than in method. Gronchi operated openly. He unhesitatingly made public speeches and wrote letters that clashed with the official government position. Nothing in the Constitution required him to clear his speeches and letters with the Prime Minister. In a public speech, he indirectly chided his own government by suggesting that a distinction needed to be made between solidarity with the West and subservience to the West, the "blind adherence to the opinions of others." [12]

Although Gronchi had been a Christian Democratic parliamentarian and party leader, identified with the left wing, his power did not come primarily from this connection. He had few followers among the Christian Democratic parliamentarians and party officials. His relations with Fanfani were both friendly and hostile, and his election to the Presidency was engineered against Fanfani's wishes. Pietro Nenni, with whom Gronchi had had close relations, effectively maneuvered him into the Presidency by working with dissident, right-wing Christian Democrats to sabotage Fanfani's choice. Perhaps Gronchi's most important source of strength, outside the presidency, was his relationship with the left-wing Christian Democrat Enrico Mattei, head of the National Energy Trust (Ente Nazionale Idrocarburi, or ENI). Gronchi also had connections with the Industrial Reconstruction Institute (Istituto per la Ricostruzione Industriale, or IRI), the state holding corporation, which owns a controlling interest in a large number and variety of Italian industries.

Gronchi could make use of certain functions of his office that do not necessarily require direct government approval. Personally making state visits, sending representatives to formal ceremonies in other countries, are in the twilight zone where acts can be either official or unofficial. For example, Gronchi sent Florence's Mayor La Pira to Morocco as his personal representative at the coronation of the late King. La Pira spoke to the Moroccans about oil concessions for Mattei's ENI and paved the way for Mattei to visit Morocco later. All this was done outside the Foreign Office. Some opponents charge that Gronchi forced approval of his visit to the Soviet Union in early 1960 with a veiled threat that otherwise he would go without government consent. The Cabinet finally agreed to the visit, and the President made the trip, accompanied by Foreign Minister Pella.[18]

The President can make his views felt through personal contact and suggestion. Gronchi felt that because he was head of state, the ambassadors represented him, and he conferred with them (some claim that he instructed them) before they departed for their posts abroad. On their return to Rome, they reported to both him and the Foreign Minister. Gronchi may have come close to usurping the Foreign Minister's functions, but nothing in the Constitution says that the ministers must be the President's only source of information.

The President can make suggestions to the ministers, and apparently Gronchi did not hesitate to do so. Among his wide-ranging ideas: the Italian Government's agreement to a visit from President Nasser of the U.A.R. (which did not materialize), and the so-called Pella plan for aiding Middle Eastern countries by employing the repayments the Western European countries were making on money borrowed from the United States (the latter rejected this plan).

Gronchi, unhappy about what he regarded as Italy's inferior position in the Atlantic community, did not hesitate to make public statements favoring Latin blocs, Continental blocs, Mediterranean blocs—all, naturally, conceived as compatible with the Western alliance. These statements usually coincided with state visits. Gronchi felt that Italy suffered in the Afro-Asian world by being identified with France and England in the Atlantic bloc. Above all, he envisioned for Italy a mediating role in East-West relations and European-Arab relations—a mission of peace, a mission of civilization. However, the brusque treatment that Moscow accorded him in early 1960 probably made him more realistic about Italy's possibilities. In any case, there is little evidence that he was a neutralist or that his criticism of specific aspects of the Atlantic Community stemmed from a desire that Italy withdraw from it. And, despite the many remarks by political enemies about his "sinister" power, that power was considerably limited. With a weak Christian Democratic Party leadership, the Cabinet and the ministers become less effective and other individuals and groups become more so. Any President gains strength in such a situation. In May, 1962, Antonio Segni was elected President of the Republic. It is too early to judge his impact on the office. As a former Prime Minister and Foreign Minister, however, he may face considerable temptation to intervene actively in the processes of making foreign policy.

6

THE CHURCH

The Catholic can never overlook the teaching and the instruction of
the Church; in every field of his life he must base his private and
public behavior on the guidance and instructions of the hierarchy.
                              —L'Osservatore romano [1]

Everybody runs to the priests, to make use of their backing in
relations with the powerful, and thus a tiredness is produced in the
country toward the men of eternity, transformed into agents of temporal things. This is not the way to honor the Church. This, rather,
dishonors it. This is not serving the Church, this is using it.
                              —ALFREDO CARDINAL OTTAVIANI [2]

The power of the Church in Italy is primarily materialistic rather
than spiritual. Everybody runs to the priests because everybody believes that the priests produce results. If the priests had not transformed themselves into agents of temporal matters, the laity would
not run to them. Spiritual influence cannot be measured directly.
Its presence or absence may be disclosed by the atmosphere prevailing in a society, by the morals and manners of the laity and the
clergy. As pointed out earlier, Italian society is highly materialistic
and, in certain aspects, corrupt. This is not merely the judgment of
puritanical outsiders, but also that of qualified Italian observers.
Before his death, Don Luigi Sturzo, founder of the Christian Democratic Party's predecessor, the Popular Party, had been engaged in an
essentially fruitless campaign for the "moralization" of Italian life.[3]
The Socialist Pietro Nenni described the public attitude toward
politics in pessimistic terms: "The old Roman and Italian skepticism
helps to reinforce the feeling that white, red, black are all the same

thing and that the public administration is by definition and by natural function a trough." [4] Cesare Merzagora, Christian Democratic President of the Senate, denounced the "atmosphere of corruption [that] weighs on Italian political life, polluted by speculation and unlawful financial activities." [5]

Even in a country that is nominally more than 99 per cent Catholic, determining Church influence on human behavior is almost impossible. True religiosity cannot be revealed by statistics. Political obedience is not necessarily a test. Before the 1958 general election, the Italian Bishops' Conference issued a "sacred notice" calling on all voters to "vote united" for the Christian Democratic Party.[6] The party received 42.6 per cent of the votes, but this can hardly be taken as the percentage of the population that is religious. Yet, the Church and its organizations are more powerful today than at any time since unification. This says little. Anticlerical governments dominated Italian political life before Fascism came to power. After Mussolini's grand "reconciliation" with the Vatican in 1929, his position, while it did not make him completely immune to Church influence, certainly gave him substantial independence.[7]

Even under De Gasperi, the Church was held at a distance. At times, relations between Pius XII and the Prime Minister became quite strained. After the sweeping election victory of 1948, which gave the Christian Democrats a majority in both houses of Parliament, the Vatican wanted a one-party clerical government installed and the Communist and Socialist parties outlawed. De Gasperi refused, and formed a coalition government with lay parties—Liberals, Republicans, and Social Democrats. In 1952, the Catholic Action Society exerted strong pressures to tie the Christian Democratic Party to the Monarchists and Fascists. De Gasperi again refused. He could do so as long as he was successful in politics. But in the 1953 election, the Christian Democrats won only 40 per cent of the vote and this eliminated De Gasperi, the last really strong man in the party.

After 1953, the Church markedly expanded its influence in political and administrative affairs. Former Prime Minister Ferruccio Parri declared: "In the judgment of authoritative Christian Democratic Party exponents, never has the interference of the ecclesiastical authorities in the administration of the state and of the large parastatal entities such as the IRI been so open, insistent, systematic." [8]

This influence is exerted in infinite ways, most of them informal and private. Least important is formal representation of the Vatican Secretary of State through diplomatic channels. The degree of influence varies and is the subject of dispute. The pressure exerted by the principal lay organ of the Church, the Catholic Action Society, probably has been overrated.[9] Direct pressure from a bishop is more important, and at least one writer claimed that practically every bishop was temporal boss of his diocese.[10]

Church interest in temporal affairs extends to personnel. In a country where the right "recommendation" is crucial in obtaining a position, the support of a bishop or his representatives may be decisive in getting a post in a private or public bureaucracy, and even receiving a Christian Democratic Party nomination for elective office. Every Christian Democratic politician maneuvers to have his picture taken with a high cleric or to give the impression that he, and not another Christian Democrat, has the endorsement of a certain cleric. If attacked by a Church official, a Christian Democratic politician will make it his business to be seen prominently with an equally high cleric within a couple of days.

With individuals thus beholden to them, the clerics have become major channels of pressure as well as liaison agents for those seeking favors. A walk down the hallways in numerous ministries in Rome will disclose the many priests approaching bureaucrats on behalf of businessmen, favor seekers, job seekers, etc. To a considerable degree, the bishops have supplanted the deputies and senators in this role.

Churchmen have access to all parties, including the Communist, and to the business community as well. Many members of the black (papal) aristocracy hold important positions in banking, real estate, and industry.[11] The Vatican has funds invested in many areas of Italian business, and owns a controlling stock interest in a number of large firms. Through lay associates, it is connected with large investment and holding groups.[12]

The informal channels through which influence flows makes it difficult to measure its effectiveness, except by the weak, sometimes unreliable method of circumstantial inference. We know that access is not influence. We know that demands and requests for favors decrease in effectiveness the more they are repeated. Despite open

Church intervention in the 1959 elections, the Christian Democratic Party failed to hold two regions, Sicily and the Val d'Aosta.

Yet in the spring of 1960, Vatican backing enabled a minority of executive-bureau and parliamentary Christian Democrats successfully to resist the majority decision to negotiate for Socialist support for a Center-Left government. On May 17, 1960, *L'Osservatore romano* attacked this "opening to the left" as contrary to Catholic doctrine. The editorial made the point, however, that "collaboration with those who do not admit religious principles may arise. In that case, it is up to the ecclesiastical authority, and not to the choice of the individual Catholic, to decide on the moral lawfulness of such collaboration. . . ." [13] The Church can ignore its own doctrine, but the lay politician cannot. From evidence of this kind, plus rumors and indiscretions, we infer the existence of sufficient influence to determine the kind of government coalition that will be formed. For by inference the Vatican, at the least, did not object to the subsequent government formed by Fernando Tambroni in April, 1960, with the votes of the Fascists.*

It does not necessarily follow that the power to make or break governments is the power to make or break foreign policy. There is little evidence of Church efforts to interfere in routine operations of the Foreign Office. Its hallways are relatively free of clerics, except in the emigration section. The Church has tried to influence the appointments of ambassadors or to get young men into the career diplomatic service, but these appear to have been scattered instances.

In fundamental policy orientation, there can be no question of Church influence on the government's attitude. Here it is impossible to speak of a collective abstraction called the Church, or the Vatican. The preceding discussion has done this for the sake of convenience. But there is no single Church or Vatican viewpoint on Italian policies, domestic or foreign. Rather, there are the attitudes of individual high prelates or groups of prelates. These opinions may vary slightly or substantially. They may be deep or superficial, emotional

---

* Of course, the Fascists claim to be good Catholics, but it is not necessary to take them at their word. For other evidence of ecclesiastical intervention in Cabinet-making, see Ignazio Silone's charge that the Fanfani government was broken by bishops inside and outside the Vatican in January, 1959. He named Cardinals Tardini and Ottaviani among others. Silone, "Apparati, religione, e politica," *Tempo presente*, March, 1959, p. 228.

or calculated. Following the thread of their effect on government policy is much like the guesswork and speculation of U.S. analysts trying to fathom the political forces at work inside the Presidium of the Communist Party of the Soviet Union. But in spite of these obscurities, the attempt must be made.

The impact of the Soviet Union outside Italy and of the Communist Party inside Italy have been fundamental factors influencing Church leaders. They regard the Communist philosophy and economic system as less dangerous than the political and military power of the Communist world. In 1922, the Vatican Secretary of State, Cardinal Gasparri, stated:

> The Church . . . is completely agnostic and indifferent to the various forms of an economy. Its spiritual interests are above and beyond economic systems and can be protected in any kind of political and social climate. It asks only that the organs of the state, of any kind, do not place obstacles in the way of, and do not attempt to undermine, the free development of religious and sacramental life, in which is found the competence and ministry of the Church.[14]

This attitude gradually stiffened, and by 1930 the Church was firmly opposed to Communism and the Soviet Union.[15] Pope Pius XI, in his encyclical *Divini Redemptoris,* declared that "Communism is intrinsically perverse." This attitude continues. Yet it would be wrong to conclude that accommodation between Church and Communism is impossible. In the nineteenth century, Pope Pius IX, in his Syllabus of Errors, took a similar attitude toward liberalism. Nevertheless, his successors managed to accommodate themselves to liberalism both inside and outside Italy. Accommodations have been made with Fascism and Nazism, and even with Social Democracy, which has not denied its Marxist origins. These accommodations, of course, have been pragmatic rather than dogmatic, for the modernist movement inside the Church was effectively crushed by Pius X.*

In World War II, Communist, Socialist, and Catholic parties col-

---

* On April 17, 1960, *L'Osservatore romano* warned that the diluted and revised version of socialism enunciated in 1959 and 1960 by the German Social Democratic Party was still irreconcilable with Catholic doctrine. This has not precluded coalition governments between Catholic and Socialist parties, as in Austria.

laborated in the resistance movement. In Italy and France, they collaborated in the government until 1947. The developing Cold War found groups in the Vatican and the Italian hierarchy divided in attitudes and policies. Similar divisions appeared among groups in Catholic political circles in Italy. The U.S. invitation to Italy to join the North Atlantic Treaty Organization brought these divisions to a climax.

Some circles in the Vatican and among Christian Democrats were swept up by the possibility of making Italy a vast, neutralized bomb shelter. Groups of Catholics associated with the journal *Cronache sociali*, whose most prominent leaders were Giuseppe Dossetti and E. Minoli, opposed the Atlantic alliance.[16] De Gasperi himself was hesitant about NATO. His doubts reflected those of Vatican prelates, such as Monsignor (now Cardinal) Montini of the Vatican Secretariat of State, and it was said that even Pope Pius XII had misgivings.[17] Sforza, after resolving his own reservations about the Atlantic orientation, persuaded De Gasperi of its necessity. De Gasperi still had to overcome the objections of other Christian Democratic leaders.[18] These were serious enough to compel De Gasperi to do something he hated to do: ask for direct clerical intervention. He took Sforza to see Pius XII, brought the Pontiff around, and thereby overcame much of the intraparty opposition.

Catholic opposition to NATO was centered in the left wing of the Catholic spectrum. These left-wing groups were against dividing the world into blocs, but were not necessarily against a movement for European unification. They deplored the aggravation of international tension and the Cold War, and favored *détente* and international pacification and collaboration. Most importantly, the group of the *Cronache sociali* saw a relation between pro-Atlanticism as a foreign policy and reaction as a domestic policy.[19]

Opposed to these groups were the right-wing elements in the party and the Vatican. They supported Cold War to the limit and close association with the United States, internationally, and a Center-Right orientation, domestically. The late Cardinal Tardini, also of the Vatican Secretariat of State, was considered the leader. The dominant Vatican line from 1950 on called for no war, no *détente*; for intransigent hostility to any efforts at negotiation or settlement between the Western and Soviet blocs. This line became centered in a group of cardinals whom the former priest Carlo Falconi has called "The Pentagon." Its most vocal spokesman is Cardinal Ottaviani. Associated with this foreign-policy line was an equally vigorous objection to the opening to the left in domestic politics. The editorial in *L'Osservatore romano* entitled "Basic Principles," of May 17, 1960, is presumably the work of this group and has been attributed to Cardinal Ottaviani.

But not all leading officials of the Vatican Curia followed this line unwaveringly. High prelates saw an increased danger of war in an atmosphere of intense and unremitting international hostility; conceivably, an accidental spark might cause a conflagration. Some bishops connected with the Congregation for the Propagation of the Faith opposed identifying the Church with the Western bloc, the colonial powers of Europe, and discredited Asian politicians such as Syngman Rhee and Chiang Kai-shek.[20] They found the missionary work of the Church hampered in Asia and Africa, the center of neutralism, by an image of Vatican–Cold War, Vatican–Atlantic bloc. Pope John XXIII attempted to offset this image in an address to the second World Congress of Negro Writers and Artists, held in July, 1959, when he said, "The Church, you know, does not identify itself with a single culture—not even with the Western culture with which its history is so closely bound—because its mission is on another plane, that of the religious salvation of man." [21]

Some clerics concerned directly with the Church's work in Eastern Europe also question an intransigent Cold War line. They have a responsibility to the faithful within the Soviet bloc, who are the immediate sufferers of an atmosphere of unbridled hostility. A *détente* contains the possibility of a relaxation of Communist pressures and restrictions, of an opportunity for expanded work and contacts for the clergy behind the Iron Curtain.[22]

The changing international situation in the late 1950's evidently led Soviet leaders to feel that some sort of relation with the Vatican was not impossible. Lithuanian bishops and laymen were permitted to visit Rome in 1958 and to report on their life and work inside the Soviet Union. In the winter and spring of 1957–58, unofficial Soviet approaches were made to the Vatican, suggesting the possibility of formally declaring Vatican City and a surrounding area of about thirty miles in radius open and safe territory, to protect the Vatican.

These approaches were not rejected out of hand, although no formal agreement was forthcoming. Obviously, neutralizing Rome and its surroundings to protect the Vatican would, in effect, neutralize the capital of the Italian state, located in the center of Italy. This would profoundly affect the Italian political atmosphere, with repercussions on the policies of the Italian Government.

The progress of an international atmosphere of *détente* coupled with the exchange of visits of heads of states and governments caused grave concern among the intransigents in the Vatican. Announcement of Premier Khrushchev's visit to the United States in 1959 resulted in a series of critical unsigned editorials in *L'Osservatore romano*. The peak was reached in Cardinal Ottaviani's attack on the "men of high responsibility in the West . . . who say that they are Christians . . . [but] shake the hand that slapped Christ in the face." [23] His direct target was President Gronchi, who was about to leave for Moscow; his indirect target was President Eisenhower.

What is being defended here? A moral code, a way of life? Undoubtedly this angry attack is motivated in part by moral outrage at the presumptions and behavior of Communist societies. But this is hardly the whole reason, for other outrageous moral systems have existed without stimulating such violent reactions from the Vatican. Hostile critics have argued that the intransigents' primary concern is the Church's material patrimony, *la roba*. This is bound up with a network of business and financial interests inside and outside Italy,[24] which ties their foreign-policy and domestic-policy lines together.

I believe that the desire to preserve political power more than any other reason produced the policy line of intransigent Cold War. In Italy, the defense of this political power is the requirement for survival as a secular, as distinguished from a spiritual, institution. For the Catholic Church, as for other large scale bureaucracies, survival is the highest value. Preservation of the base is the first goal. It is more important to hold the base in the West, and in Italy, where the Church historically has been centered, than to make progress in Eastern Europe, in Asia, or in Africa.

Experience has taught the Church that its political base in Italy has been best protected in an international atmosphere of heated tension. After World War II, it linked its political fortunes in Italy with those of the Christian Democratic Party. The party's greatest success came in the 1948 general election, a few months after the Communist coup in Czechoslovakia; in the resulting international climate, the Christian Democrats won an absolute majority in both chambers. Ever since then, the intransigent wing of the Catholic spectrum has tried to re-create this atmosphere, especially in pre-election campaign periods. The subsequent election propaganda of the Catholic Action Society has reiterated the Cold War theme, picturing its opposition as Russian tanks in Czechoslovakia, Hungary, Berlin, and Poland, not the Italian Communist Party.

Not all churchmen support this approach as the best means of survival. The Church has never committed itself irrevocably for or against a political party, a political, social, or economic system, or a state or group of states. It has not always insisted that its opponents must openly capitulate. The possibility of an accommodation with the Communist world cannot be excluded, although the terms would be difficult to anticipate. Father Robert J. Graham speculates that "as the price for peace, the Holy See may not perhaps demand the abandonment of official atheism, but it legitimately may ask for a certain toleration in Russia and an end to religious subversion abroad." [25] However, it would be impossible now to provide evidence of a shift toward accommodation at the international level.

Inside Italy, the domestic parallel of the intransigent attitude has been challenged in clerical as well as secular circles. The editorial on "Basic Principles" in *L'Osservatore romano* quoted Pope John XXIII in its attack upon lay Christian Democrats who advocated an opening to the left contrary to the position taken by the highest Church authorities. But the editorial attack was directed at the violation of doctrinal discipline, not the political objective. The editorial did not exclude the possibility of the ecclesiastical hierarchy's agreeing to such a collaboration. This very point was emphasized in a personal letter sent at the end of May, 1960, by Cardinal Archbishop Montini to the priests of his Milan archdiocese. The contents were publicized in the Italian and international press. Cardinal Montini made it clear that he opposed the opening to the left "in the present moment and in the form now in prospect," and referred to insufficient guarantees for Catholic interests and honor.[26] But the tone and content clearly indicated that such an opening could very well occur with a change in circumstances and terms.

Cardinal Ottaviani's strictures did not prevent President Gronchi from making his formal state visit to Moscow. The hostile editorials in *L'Osservatore romano* did not prevent the Italian Government from following the Anglo-American lead in working for a *détente* prior to the abortive summit conference of May, 1960. Not even publication of the editorial "Basic Principles" silenced the disputing factions of the Christian Democratic Party. Those groups opposing the opening to the left seized upon the editorial to reinforce their position. Those groups supporting such an opening found in Cardinal Montini's letter some encouragement to continue pursuit of their objectives.

Many Catholic politicians, aware of the divisions in the clerical hierarchy, are encouraged by them to pursue goals that they know may offend some members of the Vatican Curia or the Italian episcopacy.* A few Italian Catholic politicians, however, resent being treated as minors, forbidden to choose their political orientations, constrained to obtain clearance from the hierarchy before they can negotiate for political alliances. But not many within the Christian Democratic Party would openly assert such independence, for neither an individual Christian Democrat nor the party as a whole could survive disavowal by the Church. On the other hand, the Church has no real alternative to the Christian Democrats and must suffer their occasional political disobedience. For example, in spite of public condemnation by Cardinal Ruffini and the entire Sicilian episcopacy, the Sicilian Christian Democrats accepted Socialist support in 1961 in order to obtain a majority in the regional legislature. No public reprisals ensued. In the fall of 1961, the left-wing Christian Democrats engaged in another drive to form a Socialist-supported government. During this time, the Italian Episcopal Conference met and made no public statement about the move. There was no point in risking an open show of disobedience.

There is some slight evidence that the Catholic Action Society may henceforth reduce its gross intervention in Italian politics. In addressing Catholic Action leaders in December, 1961, Pope John

---

* For example, in 1959, Silvio Milazzo split the Christian Democratic Party in Sicily, thus openly challenging Cardinal Ruffini, Archbishop of Palermo. He knew that he would have the covert support of some other Sicilian bishops and priests, happy to spite the Cardinal.

XXIII emphasized their spiritual rather than political function. This viewpoint was repeated in a *L'Osservatore romano* editorial that called for subordination of temporal objectives, including political and social ones, to supernatural ends.[27] By 1962, it appeared that Pope John XXIII was shifting the focus of Church attention from politics to broader questions involved in the Second Vatican Council, which convened in October, 1962.

Neither the Church nor the Christian Democratic Party speaks for all Italians. There is a long lay tradition in Italy. Even within the Christian Democratic Party, the lay tradition has roots. De Gasperi exemplified this tradition. So would, in all probability, another strong Catholic political leader. It is the absence of such strong leadership that has enabled the Vatican, as it has the President, to assume a role in Italian policy-making.

7

OTHER PRESSURE GROUPS

THE BUSINESS ORGANIZATIONS

Roberto Ducci, a career diplomat, writes: "Europeans recognize
. . . that he who pays the piper has the right to call the tune." He
observed further that "from the Magna Charta on, the power of
parliaments resided not in the faculty to speak freely against the
kings or governments or in favor of them, but in the power to con-
cede or refuse the financial means which they needed." [1]
The Italian business community is highly concentrated. A small
number of firms dominate the national market and possess most of
the capital. The economist Giovanni Demaria makes this analysis:

> In Italy, there are today about 26,000 incorporated firms. Of these,
> just 171 possess a combined capitalization that can be estimated as
> equal to 5,600 billion of today's lire. The other 25,829 corporations
> possess in all a smaller capitalization, which can be estimated at only
> 5,000 billion lire.[2]

But only ten firms have a major impact on the national political
scene. More correctly, these are not firms but groupings of firms in
the same or related industry. Each of the clusters centers around a
principal firm. These groups fall into two broad categories of companies—privately owned and state owned. In the first category are
the following, which are listed along with their principal products
and their key officers:

Fiat	Motor vehicles	Valletta
Edison*	Electric power	De Biasi, Valerio
Adriatico*	Electric power	Cini
Montecatini	Chemicals	Faina
Pirelli	Rubber	Pirelli
Italcementi	Cement	Pesenti
Snia Viscosa	Textiles	Marinotti
Falk	Machinery	Falk

* Now in the process of being nationalized.

The state firms include two broad groups:

| IRI (Industrial Reconstruction Institute) | Various | Petrilli |
| ENI (National Hydrocarbons Trust) | Petroleum, energy, chemicals | Boldrini |

Italy's banking industry is mainly government owned. About 70 per cent of the banking business is done by three categories of government-controlled banks—the IRI banks, the banks of public law, and the savings banks (*casse di risparmio*). The remaining 30 per cent is done by privately owned banks—the popular banks owned by many small stockholders, and some private banks owned by a few large interests. The bankers as a whole are not the dynamos that the industrialists are, and the state-controlled banks have been run like private operations, closely associated with private businessmen, sharing their attitudes. The same can be said of many administrators of IRI corporations, who have private stockholders on their boards of directors although the government owns the controlling stock interest.[3]

The concentration of power in the Italian business community is paralleled by a concentration of power within the firms.

The owner-manager sees to everything, if not personally, with the aid of courier-reporters, and this is often done with an attitude of dictatorial beneficence. Workers and staff members alike are considered much like wards, to be assisted even in personal and private affairs, in a process involving overmuch bowing and scraping. The result is almost no one dares question or make decisions, nor, indeed, does he want to, for it is generally understood, if not felt, that the employer's decision is at once wise and inscrutable.

. . . .

. . . those in middle and lower ranks . . . are, for the most part, little more than couriers for top management, transmitting orders and seeing that they are executed. In the process they have to protect their own precarious positions in which they have neither real responsibility nor real authority.[4]

Italian industry is organized into many trade associations and local chambers of commerce. These are brought together in one large national association, Confindustria, the Confederation of Industry. Neither Confindustria nor the trade associations appear to have much power, although ministerial bureaucrats seem to pay more attention to the trade associations than to Confindustria.[5] Both can be used for certain purposes, such as providing a mechanism whereby the large firms can keep the small ones in line, or making formal statements and providing formal representation at meetings. The actual power lies in the firms themselves, and the top leaders of these firms have no intention of yielding any of their authority to either subordinates or spokesmen.

Industry has varied means of influencing political policies. Let us turn first to the press. The newspaper business in Italy, as elsewhere, is a big business requiring big investments. The peculiarity of the Italian press is that most newspapers are owned not by firms chiefly engaged in the newspaper business but by firms engaged primarily in other businesses—automobiles, textiles, sugar, banking, agriculture, etc. These firms look upon their papers as instruments for promoting their major interests. The same, of course, can be said of the party press and the Church press. A student of Italian journalism, Ignazio Weiss, has estimated that daily newspapers controlled by industrial, financial, or landowning groups have about 70 per cent of the circulation. Journals controlled by parties of the Center or Right and Catholic organizations have about 10 per cent; those controlled by the Left, about 14 per cent; and those with ownership unidentified but not of the Left, about 6 per cent.[6]

The influence of business and industry through the daily press is limited by the low level of literacy and the inattention to political news. It has been pointed out in an earlier chapter that a very few people are interested in and attentive to foreign affairs. The press is important not so much as a reflection of broad public opinion but as a reflection of the owners' opinions. Nevertheless, even if the political news is not followed in detail by newspaper readers, an atmosphere is created that must have some, if undetermined, influence.

Few details are available on how business influence is exerted through the financing of political parties. Italian party members do not contribute to campaign funds. Many do not even pay their dues, and the parties reluctantly overlook this lapse rather than expel them. So political parties depend on a few large contributors rather than many small ones. This would appear to give business organizations an important entrée to and power over policy. Still, this is not an uncontested situation. Foreign money probably enters Italian party coffers in various untraceable ways. It is claimed, although not conclusively proved, that funds from Catholic organizations have financed politicians and political campaigns.*

Contributions are made to protect or advance interests and can be made to a party organization as a whole or to selected factions or individuals. The commitments of the parties of the Right—Liberal, Monarchist, Fascist—to defend big business tend to assure these organizations that they will get the business funds. For Center parties, such as the Christian Democrats, Social Democrats, and Republicans, split and fractionalized, contributions tend to be made to the individual candidate or factional-group leader who can be counted upon. The Left is not cut off, however; business leaders find it expedient to take out insurance with the Socialists or Communists in return for minor favors in the present and, in anticipation of the worst, some salvation in the future. It is also argued that big business indirectly finances the Communists with the brokerage fees it pays them for arranging business deals with countries behind the Iron Curtain. The Socialists are thought to benefit from similar deals with Yugoslavia and Communist China.

But when contributions are made covering a wide range of the political spectrum, there are large differentials in the amounts

---

* Charges have been made, for example, that the Vatican relief organization the Pontificia Opera di Assistenza was diverting relief funds to the financing of political groups.

granted. The Christian Democratic and right-wing parties get most of the private money available. It is impossible to get reliable figures on the amount of money involved, but it must be very substantial because election spending is on a very large scale.

Confindustria has made unsuccessful attempts to get its spokesmen elected to Parliament, but the business groups have relied primarily on access to the administrative branch of government to further their interests. A vast network of business advisory committees exists to aid ministers and top-level administrators in formulating policy.[7] Even more important, perhaps, is bribery of high-level bureaucrats. This practice is an open secret, and the traditionally low-paid civil servant is particularly vulnerable to it. Contact is also made in state-controlled firms that have private participants, for here high-ranking bureaucrats and business leaders sit on the same board. For many of these bureaucrats, employment by a related private firm is a next logical step and a natural reward for their cooperative attitude. Jobs can also be given to a politician's relatives and friends.

An important means of general influence is by planting in the administrative bureaucracy men who will protect concrete private interests while serving as full-time government servants. This planting goes on not only in government agencies but also in various committees or commissions sent to international meetings. Felice Ippolito, Secretary-General of the National Committee for Nuclear Research, describes the struggle of the electrical industry to plant agents:

> It is a daily struggle; even for the naming of the lowest expert to a meeting of Euratom, the electrical groups insist on the right to choose a man of their complete confidence, and continually make unjust, indiscriminate, lying attacks on whoever upholds a thesis not consonant with their interests. I, also, have been accused by their newspapers of being a functionary who is an enemy of Italy only because I do not identify the interests of Italy with the interests of the Edison group.[8]

The Church is an important avenue of approach. Many medium and small businessmen make contact with the administrative bureaucracy through the priests and bishops. The big industrialists have direct access to the bureaucracy and the ministers, and need no intermediaries or recommendations. With the political parties, however, especially the Christian Democrats, the support of cardinals and bishops can be useful. Cardinal Siri of Genoa, head of the Supervisory Commission of the Catholic Action Society, has close relations with Angelo Costa, the Genoese industrialist and retired President of Confindustria.[9] Vatican representatives also sit on the boards of large firms. The Church, of course, has its own interests to protect and cannot indiscriminately disperse its limited power over many issues only marginally associated with its interests.

Unemployment gives business its major leverage in foreign affairs. A shortage of jobs, a fundamental characteristic of the economy, persists in Italy, in contrast to booming employment enjoyed by other countries of Western Europe. In Italy, the fate of even a small business is political. The shutdown or expansion of a business is of national consequence, since the loss or gain of a few hundred jobs has political repercussions. When a businessman says that a foreign-policy decision will increase or reduce the number of unemployed, he has won an almost certain victory. This still holds true even though unemployment has been eliminated among skilled workers and is now due to lack of training.

The Italian businessman, even the big businessman, appears indifferent to anything outside his company's interests. He is not concerned with the broader questions of national and international politics, and cares little about ideology, culture, and the future of the human race. He cares only about promoting and protecting his business interests. There may be exceptions; men like Vittorio Valletta of Fiat, and the late Adriano Olivetti, the typewriter and office-machine tycoon, have shown a social and political consciousness, a vision of the world that goes beyond the narrow confines of their firms, but these men are atypical.

The medium and small businessmen care only about protecting their business. The larger businessmen are divided between those who feel secure enough to go out after broader, foreign markets and those who fear international competition. The Italian economy was developed under heavy government protection and encouragement and is pervaded by fear of competition. This attitude has thus far blocked all government attempts to effectuate an antitrust and anti-monopoly policy. Such legislation has been introduced in Parliament, only to be emasculated or blocked.[10] Inattention by many medium and small businessmen enabled the government to go ahead with the Italo-French customs union in the late 1940's. When the protected interests discovered the danger, opposition rose, and, coupled with even stronger objections from French business and labor, made the customs union a dead letter.[11]

Among most businessmen, there was little serious interest in or knowledge of the European Common Market. Many owners of small firms were unaware of the negotiations. However, the heads of the larger firms, with their research sections and government-relations bureaus, directly followed and checked on these developments. The Common Market negotiations were carried on along with the negotiations for creation of Euratom. One of the principal Italian diplomats involved, Count Massimo Magistrati, commented:

In reality, it was much easier to negotiate and lay down the norms for Euratom than for the Common Market. In the former case, everything is organized for the future; in the latter, much attention and study was necessary in order not to disturb or upset too rapidly or too severely existing equilibriums and . . . vested positions.[12]

The Italian Foreign Office, like all its counterparts, is engaged in promoting business abroad, maintaining a career corps of commercial counselors to help in this, and cooperating with various tourist bodies and trade-promotion agencies from other ministries and private organizations. Trade agreements negotiated with foreign countries are handled in close association with the representatives of other ministries and the firms that will be affected.[13] The extremes to which the Italian Foreign Office will go to promote business are somewhat unusual. When the leader of a large firm makes a foreign business tour, the ambassador himself acts as guide and host.

The Italian Ambassador to Venezuela in 1957 and 1958, Count Giusti del Giardino, took even more drastic steps. The former Venezuelan dictator, Jiménez, had let out to Italian firms contracts worth some $1 billion. To get these contracts, Italian business groups had pressured the embassy into bribing key men in Jiménez's government. Then Jiménez held a plebiscite to reinforce a shaky domestic situation and pressured the Italians to round up votes for him among emigrants in Venezuela. The Italian business firms, with $1 billion in contracts at stake, put the pressure on the Foreign Office in Rome. Under the ensuing instructions from Rome, Giusti del Giardino intervened in the internal affairs of Venezuela by maneuvering the Italian emigrant community into supporting Jiménez. Jiménez was subsequently overthrown by a revolution, and the Italians in Venezuela, including the Ambassador, became very unpopular. The left-wing parties in Italy raised questions in Parliament about Italian support for Fascist dictators. They were told that the jobs of many Italian workers, Communist and Socialist workers included, were at stake, and the questioning died down.[14]

This tendency to deal with Latin American dictators until the end was also illustrated in Argentina and Cuba. It appears that Italian firms were selling arms to Perón right up to his downfall, and Fidel Castro claimed that Italian and English armaments manufacturers were the last two groups to sell weapons to Batista before the latter's overthrow.[15]

I do not imply the existence of a special favoritism toward petty Fascist dictators. Italian businessmen are equally eager to sell to Russian and Chinese autocrats and to Eastern European satellites. Trade missions will leave for Moscow no matter how tense the international situation. The late right-wing Christian Democratic senator and businessman Teresio Guglielmone actively promoted trade with Communist China and headed business missions to Peking when his own party was denouncing the Chinese Communists for bloody persecutions of Chinese Catholics.[16] The retired Monarchist senator and ex-career diplomat Baron Raffaele Guariglia also worked for economic contacts with mainland China and visited Peking for trade purposes. All Italians, from Left to Right, inside and outside the government, regard their country's refusal to recognize Red China as ridiculous and bow only reluctantly to American pressures on this issue.

In February, 1958, the Foreign Office sponsored a weekend round-table on foreign policy, inviting representatives from industry, the academic world, other ministries, etc. The industry representative, Quinto Quintieri, Vice President of Confindustria, spoke on only one subject—increased trade with the Soviet bloc. He attacked the American Battle Act, which requires the withdrawal of all U.S. aid to countries violating the strategic embargoes against the Soviet bloc and China. He asked General Marras, the retired Chief of Staff, if there was any military justification for the Battle Act. General Marras answered that there was little or none. Quintieri wanted to know what the Foreign Office could do to cut the strategic-goods list to a minimum.

This incident illustrates the fundamental aim of Italian business—to trade with anyone and any country. This has been the official government position during the postwar period.[17] Foreign Minister Attilio Piccioni expressed this outlook in a Senate speech on July 11, 1962, when he said that Italy trades with all countries, regardless of ideological and political prejudices.[18]

Obviously, Italian businessmen do not worry about an expansion in the economic activity of the Soviet world or Communist China. If they do see a threat, it appears not to interfere with their desire to make money. This driving desire leads them to exert a pressure on Italian foreign policy that has political limitations, but also political consequences. The limitations are mainly the counterpressures of United States influence on Italy, which needs United States backing. Whether Italian businessmen like it or not, their government does not yet recognize Peking, and the Battle Act, somewhat watered down, stands on the U.S. lawbooks.

Italian industrialists would like to see a general *détente* in the Cold War so they could profit from the resultant expansion of trade. Good political relations with Middle Eastern countries and Yugoslavia have paid off in increased business. After settlement of the Trieste question, Italian trade with Yugoslavia expanded rapidly, and by the end of 1957, Italy had gained first place in both exports to and imports from Marshal Tito's Communist state.[19] An Italian political journal concluded from this experience that "the consolidation of political good-neighbor relations remains an irreplaceable premise for the consolidation and expansion of good economic relations." [20]

This conclusion is congenial with the Italian business mentality. According to this way of thinking, trade takes a natural course and politics can deflect it temporarily but cannot and will not do so in the long run. It looks upon money as a principal influence on human motivation and behavior, and thinks that through money and trade the West can influence the Soviet and Chinese worlds. This viewpoint naturally plays down ideology, as illustrated by the Milanese industrialist who told me that Soviet foreign policy is fundamentally a continuation of Czarist policy.

Italian industrialists want to do business without interference from politicians or moralists, native or foreign. They are set up to do it. The major firms have special offices manned by executives who carry on diplomatic and economic relations not only with foreign firms but also with foreign governments and their foreign and economic ministries.[21] They can work through their own government—or around it if necessary. If questions of "grand politics" make it inadvisable for the Italian Government to accede to their demands, they will simply bypass the Italian Government, of which they have a low opinion. They are ready to make deals and do not regard resistance to the bitter end or the pursuit of abstract ideals as the way to survival in the national or international community.

> The money power does not ask anyone to die: It is by its nature against intransigence. It presupposes the transaction and the compromise. It does not talk about absolute principles, about dogmas. There is always the possibility of reaching an understanding, of making a deal. One has to find the right price. It disassociates the temporal from the spiritual, puts aside any fanaticism for the flag; everything that is temporal has a price: One can buy and sell. All this may be somewhat ugly, but it is always less ugly than killing.[22]

But Italian big business is caught between cross pressures. An international *détente* would improve trade relations with the Soviet world. But, it would also increase the danger that domestic enemies on the Left might come to power. This is not a theoretical danger. It is very real, and takes the form of *dirigismo*, the policy of state direction of the broad economy and state ownership of certain key sectors of the economy, especially natural resources and power. Here loom the left wing of the Christian Democratic Party and the Socialist Party as a whole, and along with them the ENI and its late dynamic leader, Enrico Mattei. Mattei was killed in an airplane crash in the late autumn of 1962 but his successor, Marcello Boldrini, has promised to continue his policies.

The ENI, a state-owned holding corporation operating in the economic areas of petroleum and its by-products, extended oil operations to the Middle East, coming into conflict with the Anglo-American oil consortium. The consortium had rebuffed Italian efforts to break into the international oil combine. In subsequent negotiations for oil concessions with Middle Eastern states, the ENI offered unusually favorable terms, which further strained relations with United States, British, and French firms.[23] It paid little heed to the Italian Foreign Office, negotiating directly with foreign governments and frequently bypassing Italian diplomatic representatives abroad. Domestically the ENI contributed to all political parties to protect its position. As an example of dynamic, efficient, and modern public enterprise, it naturally had the support of the Marxist parties, for it refuted the traditional criticism of public enterprise made by its opponents. An undetermined number of Christian Democratic parliamentarians were beholden to the ENI in various ways.

Inside Italy, the ENI extended its operations from petroleum and natural gas to chemicals, fertilizers, synthetic rubber, and electric power—which put it in competition with some of Italy's largest private industrial groups. In this competition, the ENI cut prices, a tactic previously unheard of in Italy, thereby forcing the private competitors to follow suit.

The ENI is constructing an atomic-powered electric-utility plant south of Rome and strongly supports nationalization of the electric-power industry. It is not wholly in conflict with private industry, however, and many Italian firms are its beneficiaries rather than its enemies. It even engages in joint enterprises with some of its direct competitors.

Massive expansion of the ENI inside Italy might undermine the whole economic and social structure. It is, therefore, less dangerous when it invests outside the country. This has brought it into conflict with Western firms and governments,[24] and into favorable relations with Arab and African countries, many of which are neutralist and anticolonialist in international politics. The ENI has occasionally supported its business associates against Italy's Western allies, and both Mattei and his newspaper, *Il Giorno* of Milan, were accused of taking neutralist positions.[25]

The ENI was and is first and foremost a big business, even if an unusual one. Mattei never pushed a foreign policy just on principle, nor would he risk his industrial empire by becoming too politically

vulnerable. He was capable of compromising with private industrialists, and did so. His views were not so different from theirs on foreign
policy. They were (and still are) as eager as he to expand trade with
the Soviet bloc. They are as eager as the ENI to break into Arab,
Asian, or African markets. The ENI is as interested as they in expanding into the European Common Market. The basic struggle is over
the Italian market, and in this struggle the ENI has been attacked for
its overseas operations and foreign-policy orientations because, in the
crucial domestic struggle, no holds are barred.

THE LABOR UNIONS

The simplest statement to make about the Italian labor federations
is that they are instruments of the political parties and express only
party views on foreign policy.[26] This is an oversimplification, because
the union leaders, although also party leaders, have a special concern for emigration and the mobility of Italian labor in regard to
other European labor markets. The heads of the major labor confederations are members of both Parliament and the executive
bureaus of their political parties. The largest confederation, the
Italian General Confederation of Labor (Confederazione Generale
Italiana di Lavoro, or CGIL), is led by Communist and Socialist
labor politicians; the second-largest, the Italian Confederation of
Free Syndicates (Confederazione Italiana di Sindacati Liberi, or
CISL), is led by Christian Democratic labor politicians; and the
considerably smaller Italian Union of Labor (Unione Italiano di
Lavoro, or UIL), is led by Social Democratic and Republican labor
politicians. Two other minor confederations also exist, dissident
Catholic and Fascist groups.

Like other organized Italian bureaucracies, the trade unions are
highly oligarchic, with the decision-making power concentrated at
the top. Professor Abruzzi has commented: "The unions are completely centralized in structure, organization, and power; trade-union
roads, like so many others, both originate and end in Rome." [27]

Although the syndicalist movement in Italy has its origins in nine-
teenth-century anarchist groups, it became Marxist in the last decades
of that century and has largely remained so. In the twentieth century,
the rise of a Catholic labor movement unsuccessfully challenged the

Marxist monopoly. In fact, many Catholic syndicalists themselves have a Marxist orientation. Fascism took over the trade-union movement in the 1920's. After the downfall of Fascism, the rival postwar parties agreed to avoid trade-union competition and created a single labor confederation, the CGIL, with three secretaries-general—Communist, Socialist, and Christian Democratic. However, the process of fragmentation soon began. With the development of the Cold War in the late 1940's, the Communist Party used the CGIL to achieve its own political ends, calling protest strikes against the Marshall Plan and NATO. This led to a split in 1949. The Communists and Socialists remained in command of the rump CGIL, and the Center and Right groups withdrew and formed the Italian Federation of Labor (Federazione Italiana di Lavoro, or FIL). Next, Christian Democratic abuse of the FIL caused a division, which left the Christian Democrats in control of the FIL's successor, the CISL. Meanwhile, the Socal Democrats and Republicans regrouped as the UIL.

From this chain of dismal events, the Italian workingman has benefited very little. The combination of unemployment and low wages, political domination and union oligarchy, has left the ordinary Italian workers, traditionally individualistic and anarchic, with no sense of class and trade-union solidarity. The workers do not pay their dues.[28] The unions, instead of contributing money to the political parties, depend on them for funds. This strengthens party control over the unions.

The appointment of union leaders is a matter for party politics. The party "recommendation" is required for a desirable position in the labor movement.[29] When the Communist Giuseppe Di Vittorio, one of the few top left-wing leaders who was a true son of the masses, died in 1957, his replacement as president of the CGIL and a reshuffling of its top command were negotiated by Socialist and Communist party headquarters. The Federation went through the formality of electing the successors, but this was merely a ratification of the political-party decisions already made.

The CGIL has never absolutely opposed the government's policy of promoting emigration as a partial solution to unemployment. It has, however, emphasized that it is the best of the younger Italians who get accepted as immigrants by the receiving countries.[30]

The Italian Government's failure to obtain, as a Common Market goal, the free movement of labor across national boundaries, paralleling the stated goal of the free movement of goods, originally dampened whatever limited interest the CGIL might have had in the Common Market. Interestingly, under Socialist influence, the CGIL and Giuseppe Di Vittorio early showed a favorable attitude toward the possibilities of the Common Market for the Italian labor movement. Here is the first case in the postwar period when the trade-union Communists took a line different from the Party line. Di Vittorio's heresy did not last long. Party discipline reasserted itself, and the Federation returned to the official Party opposition to Western European unification.[31]

While the trade-union Communists could not shake off Party control on even one issue, the Socialists within the CGIL, although in the minority, have continued to argue for a different attitude toward the Common Market. They recognized the Common Market's weaknesses. Riccardo Lombardi, a Socialist leader, characterized the organization as a "machine with a weak motor and strong brakes." Vittorio Foa of the Metal Machinists' Union claimed that in many respects the Common Market structure was set up by "European monopolists aiming at the preservation of these monopolists' positions." Yet the Socialists feel that it may be possible to build up a labor cartel within the Common Market to offset the business cartels. They also feel that through the Common Market the Italian labor movement could broaden its contacts with the Western labor movement and that strong Socialist influence in the six-nation group would change many characteristics of the Common Market.

Socialist persistence in this direction brought about the withdrawal of the Socialist Labor Youth Federation from the Communist-dominated International Youth Federation.[32] Foa has proposed that the CGIL withdraw from the World Federation of Trade Unions and instead take on the role of "observer" in both the Communist confederation and the International Confederation of Free Trade Unions.[33]

The Socialist union leaders have also argued that the CGIL must not be used to block economic development in Italy and that it should instead act as an independent force supporting it. In other words, the unions' actions in protecting and advancing their members' interests must be consonant with investment policies and other necessities of national development.[34] This contradicts the Communist policy of protecting workers' interests no matter what the over-all consequences.

These attitudes expressed by Socialist labor leaders are party policy; otherwise, they could not be openly presented. As deputies in Parliament, they express the party position. As trade-union leaders, they help determine that position but do not dictate it.

The rank and file care little about all this. They know only that their hopes have been abused by a leadership that has sacrificed their interests to considerations of international power politics. The resulting resentment has been felt by the leadership so keenly that in recent years the CGIL's primary objective in foreign policy has been to escape from it—that is, to avoid being drawn into disastrous political strikes. The ability to escape is limited, however, for as long as Communist politicians dominate the Federation, its interests will be subordinated, however reluctantly, to the Party's.

Socialist influence and Common Market developments have stimulated a rethinking of the CGIL's and the Communist Party's positions. By October, 1962, they both openly supported the principles of European economic integration. The CGIL has asked for representation at Common Market headquarters.

In spite of its proclaimed political independence, the CISL has been fundamentally a Christian Democratic trade-union confederation. Its top leaders are Christian Democratic politicians, members of the party's national council or executive bureau, and its former president, Giulio Pastore, has been a Cabinet minister. On general foreign-policy issues, it follows the Christian Democratic line, and this position is reinforced by the fact that the CISL as well as the UIL has been supported by Marshall Plan money and AFL-CIO funds.[35]

Since the Christian Democratic Party is essentially a collection of interest groups, the CISL has acted as a semi-independent group in the party, and has operated to preserve its own interests within the limits of obedience to the Church and the political ambitions of union leaders. It has been associated with, but not led by, the group of left-wing Catholic intellectuals known as the Sinistra di

Base, and has undoubtedly reflected some of their views on domestic and foreign issues. Whatever tendencies toward "neutralism" it might have, however—and some Christian trade unions in Europe have been accused of such tendencies[36]—have been checked by American as well as party pressure.

In recent years, the CISL has become increasingly independent of party control. It has no strong reason to assert independence in foreign-policy issues, however, as these do not concern it sufficiently except in the limited areas of emigration and the protection of workers' interests in other European countries. Without exception, its deputies and senators vote along with the Christian Democratic Party on all foreign-policy questions. Its hopes, fears, and disappointments over the Common Market are similar to those of the Socialists, described earlier. Its main concern is to avoid being dragged into political strikes. However, since it is often difficult to distinguish between an economic and a political strike, its militancy may occasionally drag it into actions that can be exploited by the Communists in the CGIL. Its good relations with Mattei assured the CISL his support in both domestic and foreign fields.

AGRICULTURAL ORGANIZATIONS

Agriculture in Italy is divided, contradictory, and uncertain. There are divisions by class, by region, by commodity. Some sections of Italian agriculture are very modern and advanced, but most Italian agriculture is backward, inefficient, and overpopulated. About 30 per cent of the Italian population still lives on the land, but most of these do not live very well. Agriculture has paid the price for past government policies of promoting, protecting, and subsidizing industry. It has been, and probably still is, overtaxed for its share of national productivity and income. Under and after Fascism, it was heavily protected and supported by government purchasing and price-support operations, which have distorted the direction of production, kept marginal producers in agriculture at minimal living levels, and provided bonus profits for the small percentage of producers who yield the major share of marketable crops.

Most landless farm laborers and a good many sharecroppers have been brought into Communist-dominated unions. The large landowners are organized into Confagricoltura, which was once the dominant agricultural group. Since World War II, however, a new organization, sponsored originally by the Christian Democratic Party, unquestionably has become the dominant agricultural organization. This is the National Confederation of Direct Cultivators.[37] It is dominated by the Christian Democratic deputy Paolo Bonomi and a few close associates. It controls the system of grain collections and prices through its control over the Federconsorzi and its influence in party councils and the Ministry of Agriculture. Bonomi claims to control more than sixty Christian Democratic deputies,[38] and he can bargain with other factions in his party to throw his support to Right, Left, or Center, depending on who will grant him what he wants.

His one and only interest is to protect agriculture and maintain high price supports for agricultural products. For example, there is now a surplus of Italian wheat, which costs more than twice the world market price. In November, 1959, the support price of wheat averaged $2.70 a bushel.[39] The coming into force of the Common Market agricultural agreement of January, 1962, will not bring down agricultural prices in Italy. The identical support prices in each member country probably will be set at a level somewhere between French and German prices, higher than the Italian.[40] In the meantime, the Italian people spend close to 50 per cent of their income on foodstuffs, and bread and macaroni products are the mainstay of their diet.

Italian agriculturalists have not objected to Italy's entry into the Common Market, since the five other countries include only one major agricultural producer—France—that is a potential competitor in the Italian market. But French agriculture is as protectionist as Italian, so there is little fear of price competition. The big danger was the entry of the Free Trade Area countries into the Common Market. Italian agriculture opposed such a move,[41] until price protection was assured in 1962. Bonomi has talked about the advantage of the Common Market in providing added markets for Italy's semitropical fruits and vegetables, but this is actually an area where the brakes are strong.

The application of strong brakes, a result of the protectionist mentality, is reflected in the thinking of the Ministry of Agriculture. The basic argument is that the peasants must be protected, because in a system with unemployment for unskilled workers, there is no place for the unemployed and unskilled peasants to go. But they are going, anyway, to swell the ranks of the squatters in the *borgate,* the slum quarters surrounding the cities of Italy, because even a high, protected price does little for them.

Relations between the Ministry of Agriculture and the non-Communist farm organizations are close. As in industry, some bureaucrats are planted in the ministry. There is a very strong influence over the nomination of the minister, and watchfulness to ensure that the Ministry of Agriculture rather than the Foreign Office dominates foreign agricultural policy. At an agriculture conference of the six Common Market countries, held at Stresa in July, 1958, the Italian delegation was led by the Minister of Agriculture. The delegation included representatives of the Direct Cultivators, Confagricoltura, and the Foreign Office.

Bonomi cares nothing about other areas of foreign policy. His organization has a monopoly on selling the agricultural machinery built by Fiat and the chemicals and fertilizers produced by Montecatini and ENI. So he will go along with his business friends as an accommodation and for logrolling purposes, supporting them in their policies and trying to avoid getting hurt in their conflicts. Meanwhile, Common Market or no, a loaf of bread and a plate of spaghetti come high.

THE INTELLECTUALS

Any analysis of the influence of intellectuals, whether as a distinct group or as individuals, must be subjective and impressionistic. Intellectuals in close personal contact with a key decision-maker may not only affect the individual's position on a specific question, but, more importantly, influence his general point of view. The question of the *éminence grise* is not negligible. The United States has had Presidents with extremely influential personal foreign-affairs advisers: Woodrow Wilson had Colonel House, and Franklin D. Roosevelt had Harry Hopkins. But American Presidents have a Congress to contend with, as well as a long constitutional and institutional tradition that restrains their freedom. The Italian Republic is very young; its institutional structure is weak; its constitutional checks are fragile and often ignored. Key individuals have unusual scope for action, and their personal counselors can consequently be of great importance.

The collective role of intellectuals can be of somewhat greater magnitude in Italy than in the United States because of the historic status of the Continental intellectual. A fair share, perhaps a large share, of the political leadership, including members of the executive bureaus, comes from intellectual workers, many directly from the academic world. The upper-level bureaucrats think of themselves as intellectuals and often write for scholarly or critical journals as well as for the weeklies. This identification with and association with intellectual circles means that attention is paid to the commentators, columnists, and writers (scholarly and otherwise) who wish to say something about public affairs.

The attention intellectuals pay to foreign affairs has decreased. The main reason is Italy's decline as a great power—but Europe itself is no longer the center of the international stage. Another reason is that Italian intellectuals must struggle for a living. This had led them to limit their attention to their own specialized fields. Commentary and written discussion of foreign affairs has tended to be confined to intellectuals who are professionally concerned— diplomatic historians, diplomatic correspondents, international-relations specialists.

To the last-named category, the leading politicians and Foreign Office bureaucrats pay some attention. Also, of course, government officials try to influence the commentators' expressions. Apparently attention is paid to the intellectuals because many areas of foreign affairs are of no direct concern to the key pressure groups, and this absence of pressure enables the intellectuals to be heard. Their voice is discordant, for intellectuals find it easy to differ and to argue. Italian intellectuals are found, in numbers far out of proportion to their small share of the population, among the small minor parties— Liberals, Social Democrats, Republicans, and Radicals—because the dominant intellectual tradition in Italian history has been the lay tradition.[42] It would be difficult to argue that the writers, commentators, and speakers exert a determining influence on the issues upon which they take a stand. They do not have access, except in individual cases, to the immediate data on which decisions are based.

Public knowledge of issues can often be acquired only after the fact. But intellectuals do affect the general atmosphere of politics, and on an issue where no immediate and direct interest is at stake, they may affect the mood or outlook of key men, even though these key men come from the large mass parties. For the mass-party leaders are more sensitive to the opinions of the political class, of which the intellectuals are a part, than they are to those of their own mass followings.

8

THE BUREAUCRACY

The Italian diplomatic corps has gone through two great crises since World War I—first because of the victory of Fascism, and then because of its defeat. The corps has survived both crises, maintaining its basic social and political characteristics. Before World War I it was an aristocratic career corps, accepting only young men of good family, often titled, with private incomes. While this background generally produced a body of men of conservative outlook and nationalistic ambitions, it did not always do so, for sections of the Italian upper classes had a liberal heritage dating back to the Risorgimento, itself a product of the liberal aristocracy and upper-middle class.

In the late 1920's, Mussolini tried to pack the lower and middle ranks of the diplomatic corps with Fascist Party hacks. However, the career people were partially successful in shunting the party appointees into consular posts rather than legation and embassy posts. Mussolini, of course, could and did make political appointments at the level of minister and ambassador—Dino Grandi, for example. On the whole, the conflict between the career people and the party people was less a conflict over goals than over style and posts. The career people, for the major part, were imperialistically inclined and nationalistically ambitious. They preferred greater caution, less crudity and flamboyance, and were well grounded in the tradition of avoiding trouble with England. They resented, naturally, the competition for promotions and assignments created by the political appointees. The Dino Grandi "line" in the Foreign Office was attractive to them; anti-German and presumably pro-British, it was not so much a product of ideological preferences as of historic traditions and geographical conditions associated with Italy's struggles for security and expansion in Central Europe and Italy's vulnerability to the British Navy. Mussolini and Ciano did not want advisers, however, they wanted servants; and the career diplomats held their tongues in order to hold their jobs. Practically none of them resigned in protest over the catastrophe that Mussolini brought upon Italy.

The next crisis came with the surrender and division of Italy in 1943. The United Nations Allies recognized the Royal Government as a cobelligerent in southern Italy, while Mussolini set up his Fascist social republic in the north behind the German lines. The career diplomats in Italy and overseas had to choose between these two competing governments, and most chose to go with the Royal Government. The diplomats stationed in Axis or Axis-occupied countries were under tremendous pressure to opt for Mussolini, but a few resisted and spent the rest of the war in Axis concentration camps.

This choice separated out the most diehard Fascists among Italian diplomats, but the choice was not necessarily based on ideological preference or a sense of moral obligation to live up to an oath of loyalty to the King. Rather, expediency dictated siding against what was by then fairly obviously a losing cause. In later years, the principal criticism made by diplomats of their colleagues who had stuck with Mussolini was not for their immorality but for their stupidity in misjudging who would win the war.

In late 1944, the Royal Government received permission to re-establish diplomatic relations with non-Axis states. The cabinets of the anti-Fascist parties composing the Committee of National Liberation appointed large numbers of political figures as chiefs of mission, including Socialists and Communists. Pietro Nenni himself was Foreign Minister for a few months in 1946 and tried summarily to retire many prewar career diplomats. After Carlo Sforza took over at Palazzo Chigi, he continued Nenni's efforts. A number of these summarily retired diplomats appealed later to the Council of State and won reinstatement.

In subsequent years, the political appointees were recalled and replaced by career people, who gradually took over the diplomatic missions abroad and the Foreign Office at home. By the end of the

1950's, only two political ambassadors were left in service. A very few political appointees have been brought subsequently into the career service. Consequently, the old career diplomatic corps is again in office. Almost all the chiefs of mission abroad, the director-generals and division chiefs in Rome, are men who entered the diplomatic corps in 1940 or earlier. Between 1940 and 1948, no examinations were held and no career appointments made. Examinations were resumed in 1948, and a new crop of younger men, an average of sixteen a year, are filling the lower ranks of the service. On the whole, they are of good family, occasionally titled, with private sources of additional income.

There are six separate directive career services in the Foreign Service: Diplomatic-Consular, Emigration, Commercial, Oriental, Press, and Central Administration services. Examinations are held separately for each. The Foreign Ministry is an exception to the overstaffing typical of Italian Government agencies, and the table of organization of each of these services is quite small. In 1957–58, the following number of positions was authorized: Diplomatic-Consular, 528; Emigration, 55; Commercial, 79; Oriental, 31; Press, 16; Central Administration, 16. In addition, a number of persons were assigned to services other than the Diplomatic-Consular, but were not regarded as having career status despite possibly several years of service.[1]

The most important service is the Diplomatic-Consular. One cannot rise very high in the others, and all the divisions are headed by members of the diplomatic corps. The table of organization for this corps is given in Table 5. The actual ranks have not been filled accordingly.

The discrepancies are shown in Table 6, which reveals the domination of the upper ranks by pre-World War II diplomats.

The last Diplomatic Annual published by the Foreign Office dates back to 1937 and gives brief biographies of the members of the diplomatic corps in 1936. The diplomats of 1957 who were in service in 1936 are found in the top five grades, although a number of councilors of embassy and of legation entered between 1937 and 1940. Among those in service in both 1936 and 1957, titles of nobility were held by five ambassadors, nine ministers first class, twenty-five ministers second class, twenty-two councilors of embassy, and

TABLE 5

TABLE OF ORGANIZATION FOR THE CAREER DIPLOMATIC CORPS

Rank	Number
Ambassador	12
Envoy Extraordinary and Minister Plenipotentiary, first class	30
Envoy Extraordinary and Minister Plenipotentiary, second class	66
Councilor of Embassy	66
Councilor of Legation	70
First Secretary of Legation	85
Second Secretary of Legation	55
Third Secretary of Legation ⎱ Attaché of Legation ⎰	144
Probationer	—
TOTAL	528

Source: Italy, Ministero degli Affari Esteri, *Elenchi del personale* (Rome: Tipografia riservata del Ministero degli Affari Esteri, 1958), p. 7.

TABLE 6

YEAR OF ENTRY INTO THE FOREIGN SERVICE OF CAREER OFFICERS

(*Serving as of 1957*)

Rank	Before 1940	After 1948	Total Number of Officers
Ambassador	11	1	12
Minister, first class	29	2	31
Minister, second class	65	2	67
Councilor of Embassy	63	—	63
Councilor of Legation	126	5	131
First Secretary	11	15	26
Second Secretary	2	42	44
Third Secretary	1	65	66
Attaché	—	35	35
Probationer	—	16	16
TOTAL	308	183	491

Source: Italy, Ministero degli Affari Esteri, *Elenchi del personale* (Rome: Tipografia riservata del Ministero degli Affari Esteri, 1958), pp. 21–76.

forty-one councilors of legation—between 30 per cent and 40 per
cent of the individuals identified.

The overwhelming number of diplomats for whom biographical
information is available studied law. A very small scattering had
majors in social science, economics, political science, or languages,
with even two in engineering. A few have two degrees. The Italian
educational system has traditionally prepared candidates for public
service through legal training. The law school of the University of
Rome has more graduates in the diplomatic corps than any other
single faculty. It should not be assumed, however, that this domi-
nance of legal training has created a legalistic mentality in the diplomatic corps. Just to live in Italy requires playing personal politics,
and building a career develops a political touch and a sensibility to
the shifting of political winds.

Candidates for the diplomatic corps must pass both a written and
an oral examination. The written examination covers five fields,
weighted equally: international law, economics, history, French,
English. No other languages can be substituted, but a knowledge of
additional languages will earn extra points.[2] The oral examination
covers the same fields plus others, including geography, languages,
sciences, and constitutional, criminal, and administrative law, as
well as observations of personal suitability. Standards are high,
especially the language standards, and the 40 per cent weight placed
on English and French together is highly significant. In the diplomatic corps, it is said, the language requirement is a substitute for
the old private-income requirement. Only candidates who have had
English and French governesses as children or have studied and lived
abroad are likely to make it. The sizable number of offspring of
career diplomats who appear in each entering class is partially the
result of language proficiencies acquired while living abroad.

Another explanation is, of course, connections. Most of the ex-
aminers are not diplomats but academic specialists grading the papers
in their particular fields. High officials of other ministries are also on
the examining board. The written examination is supposed to be
foolproof, with the graders ignorant of the identities of the fifty to
sixty candidates. It is the one examination in Italy that is reputed to
depend on merit alone. I can only repeat the observation of one
academician who said, "I know the diplomatic examination is sup-

posed to be beyond influence. If it is, it is the only one in Italy, and I still don't believe it."

The diversity of knowledge required to pass the examination cannot be acquired in the standard degree programs of any faculty in an Italian university. Practically all candidates have to spend at least two years in full-time postgraduate study. There are cram schools for this purpose, and the Bologna Center of the School of Advanced International Studies of Johns Hopkins also accepts a number of Italian candidates. A very few fellowships are available. Only "have" families in Italy can afford to finance their sons through these extra years of study. Although the examination can be taken more than once, it seldom is. Too much loss of face is suffered in not making the grade.

Entry into the diplomatic corps assures a lifetime career. No one has ever failed to survive the eighteen-month probation period, spent on assignment in the Foreign Office in Rome. During the early stages of his career leading to first secretary, the young diplomat will be promoted regularly because everyone is always rated by his superiors as excellent, unless he commits some *gaffe*. Therefore, the important thing is to avoid sticking one's neck out, to play it safe. Assignments to posts are made by the personnel division. The only rules are that an overseas assignment must be for a minimum of two years and a maximum of eight years. In practice, exceptions are made.

Italian personnel policy is based on the generalist rather than the specialist concept. The assignments follow the philosophy of giving each individual a fair chance in his career, with assignment to posts involving broad responsibility and posts involving detailed responsibility. He is to be located at a major post and at a minor one, to be far away from Italy and close to Italy, and to be assigned to the Foreign Office in Rome. There is no official classification of hardship posts, but the concept is recognized and the personnel division tries to be humane in this. In practice, the generalist philosophy cannot be pushed too far. The number of diplomats qualified as economists is very small, and so is the number with training and knowledge in Middle Eastern and Far Eastern affairs and languages. The Oriental service is understaffed for this reason, so that diplomats with qualifications in the culture of these regions, or in economics, are likely to be kept in posts involving the development, in fact, of a specialty.

A major hurdle in the career service is the promotion from first secretary to councilor of legation. It is necessary to apply to take a promotion examination, and the minimum requirement is twelve years of service, including three years in a consulate. The examination, made by an outside commission, was formerly a written examination but is now an examination of qualifications based on the candidate's record as revealed in his efficiency ratings, reports, and publications. If he fails, the diplomat can resign himself to being a first secretary until he retires. Actually, very few do fail the first time. A second chance is offered, but again, it is rarely taken.

From the rank of councilor of legation up, the candidates are known and promotions and assignments are made not by the personnel section but by the senior officers of the Foreign Service. Ministers and ambassadors are nominated by the President on the advice of the Cabinet. These posts do not have to be filled by career men, but, as reported earlier, in fact they now are. In practice, almost every career diplomat can count on ending his service with at least the rank of councilor of embassy. The increasing number of independent states in the world and the number of international organizations at which permanent diplomatic missions are maintained assure a career diplomat that at some time he will be a chief of mission. Since most missions require a title of embassy, the career ambassadors, the ministers of first and second class, and a considerable number of councilors of embassy will actually be posted abroad with the rank of ambassador.

The Foreign Office is organized into five direction-generals, divided into geographical or topical divisions,[3] and a number of services. The direction-generals are political affairs, economic affairs, personnel, emigration, and cultural affairs, and each is headed by a director-general. There are a number of services, for example, a ceremonial service and a press service. At the top is the Secretary-General, the equivalent of the British Permanent Undersecretary. The Foreign Affairs Ministry is the only Italian ministry to have a Secretary-General, a key career officer who centers and coordinates, when he is permitted to, the operations of the Foreign Ministry.

The emigration section operates practically independently of the rest of the ministry. It is headed by a political undersecretary, with a director-general under him. It figures in foreign policy whenever a blow-up occurs, such as the one in Venezuela. Otherwise it goes its own way, carrying on operations of a fundamentally routine character.

Internal operations of the Foreign Office are handled rather informally; personal contact is the way to get things done. There are only two standing intraministerial committees: a committee on legal claims, and an executive committee composed of the Secretary-General and the director-generals. Other committees are *ad hoc*, typically a small group of men gathered to work on a particular issue. Working papers are produced, but without the ponderous and groaning authority of American intra- or interdepartmental committees. These papers can be ignored, overruled, stopped, or modified at will by superiors.

The important point is that the superior officers, the director-generals and key ambassadors, retain power in their own hands, when permitted to do so by *their* political superiors. The oligarchical pattern of authority in the Foreign Office repeats the pattern found elsewhere in Italian society. Professor Abruzzi's characterization of the intermediate ranks of executives in the business world as "couriers for top management, transmitting orders and seeing that they are executed," applies here, too. The locus of bureaucratic power could be further limited to the Secretary-General and two director-generals, of political affairs and economic affairs. It is by these three men, plus a few key ambassadors at the major capitals, that the Foreign Office position is crystallized.

The Secretary-General can play a crucial role when permitted to do so. Communications are channeled through his office, and he decides who is to be brought in on an issue. He can bypass division chiefs or service chiefs who he knows will be unsympathetic, if not actually opposed, to his point of view. He may even try to bypass his political superior, the political undersecretary. In the absence of standing subject-matter committees, the Secretary-General can include or exclude those involved in an issue. A particular officer—the division chief of the Middle Eastern division in the political-affairs direction-general, for example—may have a claim to be consulted on a problem falling within his geographical area. It may be hard to avoid calling him into a discussion of such a problem, but it is not hard to have another discussion at which he is not present. It would be easier, of course, for the Secretary-General to fill all the key posts with his preferred confidants and associates, but he does not have a free hand; seniority, political, and personal claims check his scope. There is a keen competition for promotions and assignments among numerous upper-level career diplomats. They are divided by factionalism, which is mainly inspired by personal ambition. Membership in a lower-echelon clique is the consequence of a failure to be promoted by members of the other group. Since it is necessary to find some justification other than personal resentment for opposition to a dominant group, however, factional strife discovers policy conflicts to rationalize the replacement of one group by another.

These factions become aligned with political-party conflicts and factional conflicts within the parties. Two principal diplomatic factions have been associated with Fanfani, on the one hand, and Pella and Martino, on the other. An assignment to a particular foreign capital, especially a major capital, or to the post of director-general becomes a test of power between factions that may even involve the Foreign Minister, the Cabinet, the President, and the party executive bureau.

Under Italian law, a career bureaucrat need not be nonpolitical. He can quite openly be a party member and participate in party politics. If he wishes to be a candidate for Parliament, he need not resign from the bureaucracy. After his candidacy is formally announced, he is given a leave of absence without pay. If he is elected, his leave of absence is continued, so he can return to his career later if he should lose in the future. Getting on the ticket requires powerful political friends, and getting elected involves obtaining numerous preference votes that can be mobilized only through the support of influential leaders or factions. None of the career diplomats have run for office on the Communist or Socialist tickets, naturally, but they have run on the Christian Democratic, Liberal, and Social Democratic tickets. Career diplomats can also accept political appointment to the personal cabinets of any minister and return to their careers when the Cabinet undergoes a shake-up or falls.

Since there has rarely been a clear-cut victory among the contending factions of the Christian Democratic Party, it has sometimes been possible for a number of career diplomats to get ahead by being neutral in the factional struggle, receiving high appointments in Rome because of the impossibility of filling important posts with known factional leaders. In this manner, a number of nonentities have filled key posts such as Secretary-General or director-general of political affairs.

The ability of the Secretary-General and his principal assistants to influence foreign-policy decisions depends on the personality and the political power of the Foreign Minister. A Foreign Minister may make a Secretary-General his major political adviser, or he may make him a file clerk. The professionals usually believe that they can convert any Foreign Minister to their views in a few months, but this belief has often been belied by events. Faced with a resolute government or resolute Foreign Minister, the bureaucrats capitulate. In the presence of a weak, irresolute minister or cabinet, which the bureaucrats can almost sense by intuition, the bureaucrats resurge.[4]

The key decisions of foreign policy lie in the hands of a very few men. A couple of historical examples can illustrate this. In March, 1953, just before the general elections scheduled for June, 1953, the United States proposed, in utmost secrecy, a solution of the Trieste dispute with Yugoslavia involving the *de facto* partition of the Free Territory of Trieste on a line close to but not quite coinciding with the line dividing Zone A and Zone B of the Free Territory. The United States offered, if the Italian Government would accept this settlement, to exert its utmost influence on Marshal Tito to agree to it. Up to this moment, the official Italian position, supported by the United States, Britain, and France, was that the entire Free Territory should be returned to Italy. This position had been established jointly in the spring of 1948 to help De Gasperi win the 1948 election. The split between Stalin and Tito had subsequently made the position obsolete, but the Western powers were formally still holding to it. The current American offer was based on the hope of providing Italy with a diplomatic settlement that would aid the government in its election campaign. The American conditions were two: 1) utmost secrecy must be maintained before the Americans approached Tito, and 2) Italian acceptance must be final.

In 1953, De Gasperi was both Prime Minister and Foreign Minister. Four ambassadors—Tarchiani in Washington, Brosio in London, Quaroni in Paris, Casardi in Belgrade—and Del Balzo, the director-general of Political Affairs, wrote a memorandum to De Gasperi urging him to accept the American offer as the best Italy could get. The memorandum was supported by Zoppi, the Secretary-General. De Gasperi, a man of the frontier, a native of Trento, a former deputy in the Parliament of the Austro-Hungarian empire, could not swallow such a sacrifice. The ambassadors were recalled to Rome for consultation. For two days, the fight went on at Palazzo Chigi. Present were the men mentioned above plus the Undersecretary of Foreign Affairs, the Christian Democratic politician Taviani. De Gasperi thought Italy's position would improve in the future; the ambassadors thought the opposite. De Gasperi claimed the ambassadors had lived away from Italy too long and could not understand the reaction that would occur in the city of Trieste and inside Italy. He called his agent in Trieste, De Castro, to Rome to report on opinion in the city. Finally he rejected the offer. A few days later Tarchiani and Zoppi tried to get De Gasperi to reconsider. They failed.[5] A year later, in the fall of 1954, when De Gasperi was dead, the Italian Government settled for less.

From the point of view of emotional involvement and public concern, the Trieste issue has been the single most important foreign-policy problem in the history of the Italian Republic.[6] Surveys indicate that it is the only foreign-policy issue that has ever penetrated the villages and countryside. The simple reason is that to the Italian nationalists Trieste is not "foreign." Yet on an issue as crucial as this, one man had all the responsibility and a very few were even aware of the necessity of making a decision. Even among the few present, a number were spectators; the argument appears to have been carried on mainly between Tarchiani and Brosio, political appointees, on the one side, and De Gasperi on the other. Public opinion, the powerful pressure groups, the "grand electors," were unaware and unconsulted. If they entered the picture, they entered as images in the minds of the few participants, conflicting images, for the arguers disagreed about what the Italian people would accept. De Gasperi turned out to be the mistaken one, for the subsequent settlement provoked no public revolt or political punishment for the Christian Democratic Party.

In the early part of July, 1958, Amintore Fanfani became Prime Minister and Foreign Minister, succeeding Foreign Minister Giuseppe Pella, a leader of the opposing right-wing faction of his own Christian Democratic Party. The top bureaucrats in the Foreign Office were identified with Pella. In the week of July 17, 1958, Fanfani sent Eisenhower and Adenauer messages that were typed on his personal typewriter in his own apartment. Neither Secretary-General Alessandrini nor Director-General of Political Affairs Magistrati saw these messages, nor were their texts known several weeks later. Shortly after, Fanfani flew to Washington, taking with him as consultants his own *chef de cabinet*, Manzini, a career diplomat, and Bernabei, editor of the party paper, *Il Popolo*. Until he could put his own factional supporters into key positions,[7] he bypassed the top career men, conducting his policy out of his own office. His *chef de cabinet*, rather than the Secretary-General, became the distributor of communications and coordinator of operations. This pattern of operations is hardly unique to Fanfani; it follows a long Italian tradition.

Consulted or ignored, the diplomatic corps has a social status that is still valued and recognized, and a certain *esprit de corps* that differentiates it from other bureaucratic groups. It is the one bureaucratic group recognized as honest; it is incorruptible by money, if not by ambition. Beyond this point, outside opinion varies. Bureaucrats in other agencies have considered the diplomats stupid; academic specialists have considered them incompetent. Political opponents have considered them reactionary, if not Fascist. The former Minister of Foreign Affairs, Gaetano Martino of the Liberal Party, rose to their defense in the following open letter:

> As in every other category of functionaries, so among the functionaries of the Foreign Affairs Ministry will be found men who are excellent, good, less good, and mediocre; but it would be unjust not to recognize that, on the whole, for their moral and technical qualities they are qualified for their functions and do not merit, as they have received from some, the contempt and blame of the nation.

It is also just to recognize that, like all the other categories of functionaries, the Foreign Ministry functionaries have felt the repercussions of the extraordinary events that have harassed Italian life in the last thirty years. One would not be doing his duty to truth to maintain that Palazzo Chigi has remained an island of the past in the world of the present. I desire to render testimony not only to the professional preparation of the major part of our diplomats, but also to their loyalty and their patriotism [to the Republic].

The problem to discuss is rather another: that of the limits of the diplomats as a body of technical functionaries. The obligation to direct the foreign policy of a country belongs, in a democratic regime, to the political leaders who are constitutionally responsible to Parliament and the people, not to the bureaucracy. The functionaries are only technical collaborators. In the polemics of today, it is not easy to avoid the suspicion that an attempt is being made to unload upon diplomatic personnel the responsibilities for a policy that one does not have the courage to attack openly. . . .[8]

It would be nice if it were really as easy as Professor Martino thinks to distinguish between technical and political functions in administration, or between policy-maker and policy-executors. Modern political science knows better.

I would not be so confident as Professor Martino of the unswerving commitments to democratic republicanism of the entire diplomatic corps, although there is no question in the case of some of them who demonstrated their commitment during the resistance in northern Italy. The majority of the older diplomats are probably ideological neutrals, neither anti-Fascist nor Fascist, neither convinced democrats nor confirmed totalitarians. But one or the other, they are weak, submissive, and lack initiative. Their training period was under Fascism when Mussolini was not interested in listening to arguments or disposed to brook opposition. These are not the men to fight with their superiors for or against a policy. They are not, with a few exceptions, heroes or millionaires. If Italian policy were to change drastically, little resistance would come from them.

OTHER MINISTRIES

The Foreign Ministry is custodian of a Continental tradition of power politics that once reigned supreme. Until recently, the Foreign

Ministry could say, in disputes with other ministries, that "international political considerations require that we do such and such," or that "political considerations require that we must not do such and such," and that would settle it. This is no longer the case. Italy is no longer even nominally a great power. The requirements of foreign policy no longer have first priority, and the Foreign Ministry has found itself harried and badgered by other governmental agencies insisting on their rights, powers, and prerogatives. Since World War II, American scholars have become aware of the role of the military in foreign policy, and this awareness has resulted in a spate of research projects, institutes, and historical and theoretical analyses.[9] Such an awareness is completely absent in Italy, for the role of the military instead of expanding has drastically declined. In the words of one commentator: "The political weight of the army in our country is zero . . . ," and this judgment, shared by diplomats, politicians, and academicians with whom I have talked, is extended to the navy, the air force, and the Combined General Staff. Three-fourths of the military budget goes directly or indirectly into wages, and the main function of the armed forces seems to be to lower the unemployment figures.[10] An analysis of the army budget for fiscal 1957 showed a total budget of 264 billion lire ($422.4 million), of which 88 billion lire went into salaries and stipends, 60 billion into pensions, 69 billion into food and clothing for the troops, 26.5 billion for maintenance and acquisition of materials, and general services. For the renovation and improvement of arms and installations, only 20.5 billion lire were allotted, or 7.8 per cent of the total, the lowest of any European country.[11] Italy has relied upon the United States to provide or pay for equipping a good share of its armed forces, and from 1950 to 1960 the United States gave Italy almost $2 billion in military aid. These sums have maintained armed forces consisting primarily of twenty infantry and armored divisions, five Alpine brigades, plus auxiliary units; three cruisers, plus minor vessels; and seven air-force brigades of fighters, bombers, reconnaissance planes, plus auxiliary units.[12] Only a few units, those directly under NATO command, are up to full strength.

The history of the Italian armed forces in united Italy does not confer great prestige upon career officers or make them venerated or glorified by the people. The Italian polity has not for a long time produced any De Gaulles, to say nothing of Eisenhowers, Mac-Arthurs, or Radfords. In the early years of Italian unity, the court was surrounded by a military atmosphere, generals were a mainstay of the court party, and the armed-forces budget was high,[13] but now this is not so.

The economic ministries, not the generals or admirals, have challenged the supremacy of the Foreign Office. The Treasury has led the attack. In Italy, the Treasury must approve every expenditure, like the Exchequer in Britain. It has often withheld approval, thereby embarrassing the Foreign Office in its international relations. One example can be cited. Under the 1947 peace treaty, Italy was obligated to pay reparations to Ethiopia. For years, the Foreign Office tried to get the obligation paid, so as to restore good relations with the Negus. The Treasury, caring little or nothing about Ethiopia and under tremendous financial and political pressures at home, failed to approve payment. Other claims had higher priority.

Much Foreign Office work has an economic or commercial goal or basis, so that constant consultation with and referral to other ministries are necessary. These other ministries claim a technical expertise that gives them a basis for insisting upon their rights, and they have behind them the support of important pressure groups. In the past, delegations to conferences were led by diplomats, with the technical experts of the other ministries serving as advisers. Today, even in the negotiating process, the experts of the other ministries are supplanting the diplomats and trying to treat them as providers of services, while the experts claim the right to make the decisions.[14]

In the breakdown of all agreements concluded between Italy and other states in 1957, shown in Table 7, the predominance of economic issues can be clearly seen. Even in the categories labeled political and liquidation of claims, economic issues were involved. Certainly the Common Market and Euratom required the participation of a wide variety of ministers and private interests, and the one standing interministerial committee in foreign affairs is the committee on the Common Market.

Much of the work of diplomacy involves questions that will not

TABLE 7

AGREEMENTS CONCLUDED BETWEEN ITALY AND OTHER STATES
IN 1957

Commercial and trade		74
Emigration		13
Travel (passports, visas)		8
Political questions		8
Common Market and Euratom	5	
Armaments control	2	
Extradition	1	
Liquidation of peace-treaty claims		10
Cultural questions		3
TOTAL		116

Source: *Rivista di studi politici internazionali,* January–March, 1958, pp. 147–54.

lead to formal agreements. Nevertheless, the Foreign Office finds much of its time and personnel taken up with economic and commercial questions in which its authority is questioned, its competency impugned, and its power eroded.

9

EXTERNAL FORCES

The world in which the Italian people have lived since World War II is a product of forces to which Italy itself contributed through Fascism's adventuristic foreign policy. The war undermined historic centers of power. Postwar Italy, defeated, weak, has found both its internal security and external safety dependent on action taken by others, for their own purposes, which may or may not have coincided with Italy's interests and needs. The bipolarity of the postwar period, perhaps exaggerated by students of international affairs, has been significant enough to make the shadows of the United States and Russia loom very large on the European landscape. These shadows fall especially heavily on Italy, for the domestic social struggle brings the superpowers face to face inside the Italian polity.

The Soviet Union can try to influence the policies of a foreign government through the various means available to any modern power: diplomatic channels, political propaganda, economic and commercial pressures and attractions, military demonstrations, cultural and intellectual programs. In addition, Russia operates through the influence exerted by local Communist parties and whatever other local allies can be obtained. The Soviet Union has used all these means in Italy, but they have not prevented Italy from being among the most loyal, if not slavish, followers of United States foreign policy.

I have already mentioned the identity of positions taken by the Soviet Union and the Italian Communist Party on international issues. On only one foreign-policy matter, Trieste, were they ever in open disagreement.* From January, 1945, until the Paris Peace Conference of June, 1946, the Soviet Union supported the extreme territorial claims of Yugoslavia, while Togliatti affirmed the *italianità* (Italian character) of the city, if not of its hinterland.[1]

On domestic questions, the Italian Communist Party appears to have taken and maintained a far more independent position. It asserted and maintained, against strong pressure from Stalin, the clause in the Party's constitution that opens Party membership to all adult Italians no matter what they believe. If Stalin had had his way in restricting membership to believing and knowledgeable Marxists, the Italian Party would have a membership of 20,000 or 25,000, instead of 1.7 million. It would be an elite, cadre party rather than a mass party. Again, on the question of relations with the Catholic Church, the Italian Communists abandoned on their own account their traditional anticlericalism in favor of a policy of attempted collaboration.†

In spite of the size of the Italian Communist Party, Russia exerts little influence on the Italian way of life. Only specialists study Russian. The attraction of Communist ideology for the young intellectuals has declined sharply since the early years after World War II. Italians may be impressed by the demonstrations of Soviet scientific and technological skill and economic capability, for they respect power, but the motivational and behavioral structure of the "new Soviet man" is foreign to the Italian people (as it appears to be to the Russians, too).

The American position is different. The United States Government has exerted an intensive influence on Italian policies through

* In the autumn of 1962, the Italian Communist Party appeared to be in conflict with Soviet-bloc Parties by endorsing the Common Market. *New York Times*, October 23, November 23, 1962.

† In an article for the Communist journal *Rinascità* (November–December, 1946), Togliatti rejected the charge that the Communist Party is anti-Christian and continued: "Anticlericalism is, as an ideology, extraneous to the working class and to our party. . . . We have not wanted and do not want religious conflicts. . . . We continue to think that a vast religious conflict with an array of clerical forces on one side and a by now reborn mass anticlericalism on the other would be contrary to the interests of Italy." Reprinted in Togliatti, *Linea d'una politica*, pp. 88–94. In his efforts to appease the Vatican, Togliatti delivered the Communist vote in the Constituent Assembly in favor of Article 7 of the new Italian Constitution, which brings the Lateran Accords of 1929 into the Constitution. The Communist vote was necessary to get the article through.

all the means mentioned earlier: diplomatic, political, economic, military, cultural. In addition, there has been the role of the Italian-American and Catholic organizations.* The American presence is felt strongly in Italy in ways that go below the surface of Italian society. It is not merely the superficial and crude aspects of American life that have spread to Italy, the neon lights, the jukeboxes and pin-ball machines, the movies and television programs. Italian intellectuals may complain of the corrosive effects of American materialism, but America did not bring materialism to Italy; it was there long before. Its current form, the accumulation of consumer durables, is American in origin, for the United States developed the mass production of television sets, automobiles, domestic electrical appliances, and good plumbing.

English has displaced French as the dominant second language, and American idioms have crept into everyday Italian. American methodologies and viewpoints in pure science, social science, and education have made headway.[2] American ideas on the social emancipation of women are beginning to penetrate, especially in the larger cities.

In formal institutions, the single most striking American-style innovation is the establishment of a system of limited judicial review, through creation of the Constitutional Court.[3]

It is certainly unjustified to proclaim the Americanization of Italy, or even the pseudo-Americanization of Italy. Even the partial assimilation of a few American behavior patterns or concepts does not guarantee Italy's permanent loyalty to American foreign policy. A number of non-Western peoples have adopted several social, political, and economic concepts of Western civilization only to turn these very concepts against the Western countries. Italy will stay with America as long as Italian interests more or less coincide with American ones—but no longer.

Since the end of World War II, the interests of the dominant

* For instance, at periods prior to the Italian general elections, letter-writing campaigns were urged upon Italian-Americans and others through the Church. The opposite pressures can be exerted, too. Ambassador Tarchiani has recorded his efforts in mobilizing Italian-American communities in the United States and in Latin America to exert influence upon their respective governments in favor of Italy's position at the peace settlement. Tarchiani, *Dieci anni tra Roma e Washington*, p. 96.

groups in Italy have tended to coincide with the interests of the United States, in foreign affairs. They have both defined their security requirements in terms of keeping Soviet power out of Western Europe and the Mediterranean.[4] To reinforce this identity of interests, the United States has granted Italy large amounts of aid in various forms and over an extended period of time. Between the end of the war and 1957, economic assistance to Italy totaled $3.84 billion in grants, $744 million in loans, and $544 million in offshore-procurement contracts.[5] Military assistance was mentioned in the previous chapter. In addition, note should be taken of two American air bases in Italy, one outside Verona and the other between Pisa and Livorno, a naval base at Naples, which is the headquarters of the American Sixth Fleet, plus guided-missile bases.

American money in various forms has gone to the Christian Democratic Party and its allies. How much, the channels used, and the particular sources are subject to speculation and debate, charges and countercharges. Marshall Plan funds as well as AFL-CIO money went to the CISL and the UIL, the non-Communist trade-union federations.[6] The result was considerable American influence in the Italian trade-union movement. The CISL, if not the UIL, "has supported to the letter the foreign policy of the United States." [7] The Italian-American Labor Council, headed by Luigi Antonini of the International Ladies Garment Workers Union, has sent money to support the Social Democratic Party and its newspaper, *La Giustizia*, and has admitted sending money to the Socialist Party before the split in 1947.*

Mrs. Clare Boothe Luce, when American Ambassador in Rome, was instrumental in making it American policy to restrict offshore-procurement contracts to firms in which the largely Communist CGIL received less than 50 per cent of the vote in plant elections. The prospect of losing their jobs induced many workers, sometimes with the encouragement of the CGIL leaders, to vote for the CISL or the UIL. Thus, the CGIL lost its majority in many firms, including Fiat, the largest single industrial employer in Italy. The resultant

---

* *La Giustizia* (Rome), February 8, 1958. Oreste Lizzadri of the Socialists said that his party received money from Antonini in 1944 but rejected later offers because they were conditioned on the Socialists inside the CGIL preventing the CGIL from joining the WFTU. *Il Messagero*, February 9, 1958.

aggravation of divisions in trade-union ranks, however, was not of lasting benefit to the CISL in the Fiat plants. The weaknesses of divided labor enabled the management to split the CISL in the spring of 1958, creating in effect a company union and thereby undermining the Christian Democratic labor federation. This consequence, in the opinion of the AFL-CIO, aided the Communists, who were the original targets of the whole operation.[8]

The United States has tried to influence elections by openly warning the Italian people, as in 1948 and 1953, that continued American aid depended on the election of Christian Democratic-led coalitions. In 1948, the warning was issued by the State Department's official spokesman in Washington; in 1953, by Mrs. Luce in speeches in Milan and Genoa.[9] Mrs. Luce failed in her opposition to the election of Giovanni Gronchi as President of Italy in 1955 and in her efforts in 1955 and 1956 to prevent establishment of an oil-exploration monopoly for the ENI in the Po Valley.[10]

Although the United States and the Soviet Union are the dominant external forces operating upon the Italian state (I have preferred to treat the Vatican as an internal pressure group), there are others that deserve at least brief mention. The British role no longer remotely resembles that of the late nineteenth century, when the first principle of Italian foreign policy was to avoid conflict with England. British influence is now minor. French influence is principally cultural, although the destruction of the Fourth Republic in 1958 and De Gaulle's re-emergence as a dominant "man on horseback" produced nervous reactions in Italian democrats, who worried about the repercussions of these events on the weak, unstable Italian Republic. Germany is viewed mainly in economic terms, as a customer for Italian products and a competitor in markets in Eastern Europe, Asia, and Africa. Politically, Germany is seen mainly as a potential danger to the peace, because of its division, because of Berlin, because of fears that German irredentist demands for the lost Eastern provinces may spark a future explosion. The Italian preference in the German situation, consequently, is for the *status quo*.[11]

The Socialist International and its leading parties, the British Labour Party and the German Social Democratic Party, have had some influence on the Italian Social Democratic and Socialist parties.

The Social Democratic Party is the Italian party recognized by the International as the representative of Italian socialism. The International has been disappointed at the performance and prospects of Saragat and his followers, and the foreign parties have consequently turned more attention to Nenni, especially after Nenni's relationships with the Italian Communists became more strained. Saragat, under pressure because of the demands for Socialist reunification from the left wing of his own party, fearful of Nenni's growing appeal to the British and German comrades, has tried to maintain his position in the International by shifting his attitudes on East-West alliance policy to bring them into line with those of the British. In speeches inside and outside the Chamber of Deputies, he quotes the late Hugh Gaitskell constantly. In 1958, he reversed his opposition to a neutral belt in Central Europe when the Labourites and German Social Democrats came out in favor of it. He then backed their approval of a de-atomized zone within the framework of a continued American military presence in Continental Europe.[12] His fears for his position remained sharp, however, and in July, 1959, he openly complained that the British embassy, the Labour Party, and the Socialist International were against the Italian Social Democratic Party.[13]

The Socialist Party has undoubtedly shown much interest in the Socialist International. Nenni and other Italian Socialist leaders have informal contacts and make exchange visits with Socialist leaders of other states. The Socialist labor leaders in the CGIL have evinced their desire for increased contacts with the labor movement in Western European countries. The positions taken by British and German Socialist politicians on various questions affecting Germany, NATO, and the armaments race have been acceptable to the Italian Socialists to the point where Nenni has ceased his objections to Italian membership in NATO.[14]

How has Italy responded to these external pressures? The career diplomat Roberto Ducci was referring to the United States Government when he wrote in 1959: "Europeans recognize that he who pays the piper has the right to call the tune." He was reiterating a theme that has persistently recurred in diplomatic dispatches and letters ever since the end of the war. Ambassador Quaroni, the senior career diplomat of the diplomatic corps, wrote as early as

1945 that only the United States could help Italy and that it was necessary to "attentively avoid anything that could spoil our relations with America." [15] In 1948, he wrote from Paris: "The reality is that we, like all the other states of Europe, have ceased to be independent . . . and we are as free to move closer to Russia as Poland is free to move closer to the United States. . . ." [16] Tarchiani constantly warned in the late 1940's that economic aid granted by the United States Congress and American bankers was dependent on Italian membership in the Atlantic alliance and on an Italian domestic policy that would keep the Communists and Socialists out of the government.[17]

It may appear that the diplomats have a heightened sense of Italy's dependence. This feeling of weakness, while most acute in the period immediately after the war, appears to have abated little in subsequent years. Free and Sereno quote an American diplomat who complained, "Had the Italians been more resilient, and more resistant to our wishes, we would have had an easier time of it." [18] I myself was told in 1958 by a technician, not a diplomat, who represented Italy on a minor NATO subcommittee, that he was under instructions never to disagree with the American delegate.

The press has likewise demonstrated its sensitivity about Italy's weakness. One right-wing newspaper described the United States as the "guide and protector" of the free nations.[19] I was in Rome when Russia's first Sputniks were launched, when America's first space failures were advertised abroad, finally to be followed by the first American success. The pro-Soviet and pro-American papers could fairly be likened to two little boys shouting at each other, "My big brother can lick your big brother!"

How can we explain this Italian susceptibility, almost servility, to external power influences? Are weakness and poverty sufficient explanations? Hardly. Other European countries have gone through similar experiences, been similarly helpless, and been similarly dependent on the United States for economic survival and rehabilitation. This did not prevent them from disagreeing with the United States, often to the point of open conflict. De Gaulle, when he was most helpless and most dependent, was often most difficult.

One Italian explanation is that domestic Communism is too strong to permit Italy to enjoy the luxury of criticizing the United States.

Countries not faced with this internal threat, the argument goes, can afford to be more critical, whereas Italy must support the United States at all costs.[20] The example of France contradicts this reasoning. Communism is as strong in France as it is in Italy,[21] but this has never inhibited the Frenchmen.

A more logical explanation is offered by Free and Sereno. They attribute Italy's self-imposed submissiveness to two fundamental historical experiences: (1) a long period of subordination to foreign conquerors and rulers, and (2) the feudal lord-vassal relationship, whose psychological vestiges still persist in Italian behavior. Free and Sereno write: "The Italian tradition is to distrust governments and to be scornful of authority. But at the same time, Italians have learned through the centuries to admire and to live with power; to maneuver; to resist by evasion, but simultaneously to curry favor with the powerful ruler." [22] In addition to these causes, I would add a religious and familial tradition stressing "obedience."

This Italian posture is not peculiar to political relationships. We can refer again to Professor Abruzzi's remarks on the structure of authority in the business firm and the relationship of worker to master:

> Unless the control mechanisms are firm and ubiquitous, the Italian worker is likely to want to do things his way, particularly inconsequential things. This is not unrelated to the so-called "individualistic mentality" of the Italian, which seems to be little more than a mischievous resentment of having to yield to the will of others. Thus, the Italian worker will follow orders only if he has no choice, *and then he will follow them without protest* [italics added].[23]

Perhaps the major reason for the overcooperative posture in foreign policy is that it is considered the necessary price for relative freedom of action in domestic policy. In a reversal of the attitude of the worker just described, Italy desires freedom of action in consequential, rather than inconsequential, matters. Not that man's survival and protection against Soviet domination are inconsequential issues, but they are not subject to the control of Italian foreign policy. Over domestic affairs, the Italians do have considerable control and how they behave in this area is of consequence.

The Italians, even from the early postwar years, have resisted

American pressures in internal affairs. Tax reform is an example in the economic realm.[24] In the political sphere, De Gasperi resisted American (and Vatican) pressures to curb the Communists legally.[25] Mrs. Luce could not prevent the election of Giovanni Gronchi to the Presidency of the Italian state, nor could she block establishment of Mattei's oil exploration and production monopoly in the Po Valley.

Italy's self-imposed satellitism in foreign affairs will undoubtedly pass. The country's economic recovery and development already would have brought it to an end but for the political instability. The period from 1954, which saw the beginning of the break-up of the Center coalition, to the present can be characterized as a long transition. During this time, factionalism within the Christian Democratic Party has prevented significant domestic decisions from being taken and has produced a paralysis in foreign policy that has permitted the country to drift along with the Western world. A definitive "opening to the left," based on a stable Christian Democratic–Socialistic coalition, may see the resumption of a more active and independent, but not anti-Western, foreign policy.

III

The Future Direction of
Italian Foreign Policy

10

THE GOALS

DOMESTIC GOALS

Count Carlo Sforza, in writing of his five years as Foreign Minister after World War II, stated that "a foreign policy is only the mirror of an internal policy." [1] This statement reverses the traditional conception of the basic objective of foreign policy—the security of the state from foreign threats or aggression. Even in the contemporary world of ideological conflict, in which the notion of indirect aggression has achieved great vogue, the domestic threats to the security of the dominant elites are expected to be linked to a foreign state organizationally as well as emotionally or politically. Managing these internal threats is ordinarily regarded as a problem of domestic policy involving a choice of solutions ranging from suppression of the threat by crude force to economic, political, and social reforms that will undercut the appeal of the counterelites to wide strata of the population. Foreign help might be requested and needed in either case—to supply weapons or troops for purposes of suppression, to supply economic and political aid for purposes of stabilization or reform.

The difficulty in understanding Italian policy since World War II is that the focus has not been on the real objects of that policy. Instead, a continued hue and cry has been made about nominal threats to Italy's external and internal security. The nominal external danger has been the Soviet Union and its satellites, which possess a vast military power ever threatening to erupt and overrun Western Europe. To counter this threat, NATO was created and Italy became a member of it. But the Italians did not believe then, nor do they believe now, that there was or is a military danger from Russia. In Italy, war is considered beyond the realm of possibility.[2] In his speech to the Senate on March 27, 1949, Prime Minister De Gasperi called for Italian entry into the Atlantic alliance, but said he did not believe war was likely. He argued that Italy should join NATO to obtain economic aid for reconstruction and development. Western solidarity was necessary above all to assure Italians the right to emigrate, and this solidarity did not and would not interfere with trade with the Soviet states.[3] Whether De Gasperi was correct or mistaken, whether he deliberately minimized the danger, his line of argument had the maximum appeal for his listeners and at the same time neutralized the arguments of the opposition.

The nominal domestic threat has been the Italian Communist Party, constantly and publicly designed as the instrument of indirect aggression, linked organizationally with the Soviet Union even if the Comintern and the Cominform are no longer in existence. But it has been a long time since Italian political leaders have considered the Italian Communists a danger, even if they say the opposite in public. In his diplomatic dispatches at the end of 1948, Sforza stated that there was no Communist danger in Italy.[4]

This does not mean that Italian foreign policy is not oriented toward domestic objectives. On the contrary; *the key objective of Italian foreign policy is to protect the domestic social structure from internal dangers.* This is the basic reason for the "Western" or "Atlantic" orientation, whether it involves membership in NATO or in the economic agencies related to the several organizations of European cooperation.* In contrast, the United States regards NATO as primarily a defensive alliance against outside aggression.

The Italian concept of NATO as a protection against internal dangers is revealed in the statements of conservative governmental and political leaders and in the editorial policies of prominent conservative newspapers. Former Foreign Minister Gaetano Martino talks of the Atlantic alliance as providing the security that has "prevented the crumbling of Western Europe by intrinsic corrosion." [5] Giovanni Malagodi, Secretary-General of the Liberal Party, defined

* In 1961, Nenni wrote that NATO "was subscribed to by the Italian Parliament for reasons of domestic rather than international policy." "Where the Italian Socialists Stand," *Foreign Affairs*, January, 1962, p. 221.

the foreign policy of solidarity with the West as part of the necessary national policy against the persistent internal "Socialist-Communist threat." [6] Roberto Michelini, leader of the Fascist Party in the Parliament, announced that his party voted in favor of Italy's pro-Atlantic and pro-Western orientation in order to prevent an "opening to the left" inside Italy.[7] No one who knows the Fascists believes that they have any sympathy or appreciation for their British, French, or American allies, or for the democratic and liberal political and cultural values that are supposedly the ideological underpinnings of the Atlantic community.

The opposition of conservative groups to any *détente* in the Cold War is based on a similar premise. Prominent among Martino's arguments against a relaxation of international tension—and, perhaps, a withdrawal of Soviet troops behind their own frontiers and American troops from continental Europe—is that the West would become more vulnerable to Communist penetration which would "make it possible in six months for Communist elements within the various countries to occupy positions of predominant power." [8] The Rome newspaper *Il Tempo* argued that Italy cannot afford the luxury of a *détente* or of neutralization when it has two large combative parties such as the Socialists and the Communists. British Labourites and German Social Democrats do not face that problem.[9]

Countries with stable economic, political, and social institutions do not require defensive alliances to protect their institutions from internal threats. Communists would not come to power in the British Isles, the Low Countries, Scandinavia, or Switzerland through intrinsic corrosion or through penetration "within six months" if NATO disappeared or if a general settlement or *détente* were reached between East and West. These are socially stable societies, not dependent on foreign troops for their preservation. They might be overwhelmed by foreign conquest but not undermined by domestic penetration. They do not look upon the Atlantic community as a protection or escape from necessary domestic social and economic reform.

The Italian attitude toward the European Coal and Steel Community and toward the Common Market has a similar basis. These institutions are valued for the defense they might give to a private market economy in Italy based on the premise of *liberismo*, the reservation of economic decisions to private businessmen using indicators provided by the market. The competing concept of *dirigismo* assumes that governmental determination of broad policy objectives is necessary to eliminate unemployment and promote higher living standards for all. This can be achieved by determining the investment policies of the firms in the state-controlled sector of the economy, influencing the investment policies of firms in the private sector through governmental control of the banking and credit institutions, antitrust action where monopoly serves no public purpose, and manipulation of public spending and tax policies to achieve publicly determined goals. Banking and credit institutions are already largely controlled by the government, but they have been following purely market policies rather than social policies deliberately oriented toward development.

To the conservatives, who had predominated in domestic and foreign policy, the European regional economic institutions are incompatible with the approach of the *dirigisti*, found in the left wing of the Christian Democratic Party and the parties of the democratic left. Therefore, any Center-Left political coalition is regarded as incompatible with Italy's international commitments. Martino argued publicly that the Christian Democrats did not have the choice of making either a Center-Right coalition or opening to the left and forming a government with the support of the Social Democrats and Socialists. The treaties of the European Economic Community prohibited a policy of *dirigismo*, which would be the consequence of a Christian Democratic–Socialist collaboration.[10] He has elsewhere argued that a united socialist Western Europe would be only a step toward the extension of the U.S.S.R.'s empire. It must be a united capitalist Europe, which might include a few social services.[11] The former president of Confindustria, Alighiero De Micheli, saw in the Common Market an instrument for freeing Italian businessmen from existing "directing controls."[12] Confindustria's official newspaper, *Il Globo*, insisted that the organs of European economic cooperation have "confirmed the importance of private enterprise."[13]

We see here the attempt to use foreign policy as an instrument to preserve a highly stratified social order. The ending of unemployment and the economic upgrading of large sections of the masses would have the social and political consequence of realigning the existing power structure in Italy. Emigration would provide a partial deterrent to this consequence. The Common Market could be another, not only by providing arguments for the *liberisti*, but by providing an alternative to the necessity of drastically expanding domestic consumption in order to absorb the increasing production of Italian industry. Economic expansion might even be slowed down to avoid unpleasant noneconomic consequences. Professor Joseph LaPalombara reports what he considers reasonable suspicions that many owners probably forgo profit increases by refraining from greater productivity so as to preserve existing social stratification.[14]

Any time a Christian Democratic politician wants to consider an alliance with parties to his left, the whole right wing of his party immediately accuses him of endangering Italy's international relations. This happened in the summer of 1958, when Fanfani formed a short-lived coalition with the Social Democrats (although Saragat, of all people, has been a faithful supporter of the Atlantic orientation).[15] When talk of a real opening to the left, a Christian Democratic–Socialist collaboration, became serious, the right wing of the Christian Democrats and the whole right sector of the Italian political spectrum charged that Italy's basic foreign policy was threatened, that Italy would be separated from the Western camp. This was nonsense, and knowledgeable Italian and foreign political leaders knew it. Nenni had said so. It was this collaboration, not the Communists, that threatened the Italian social structure and power structure. To prevent this combination, foreign policy, religious dogmas, anything, was used.

In 1949, the PSI voted against Italy's entry into NATO. Since that date, the Italian Socialist Party has come a long way. In 1949, Pietro Nenni recalled in the Chamber of Deputies the historic neutralist tradition of Italian socialism, stating, "We repeat against the Atlantic pact the struggle our predecessors fought for thirty years against the Triple Alliance." [16]

In pre-election interviews in May, 1958, the Socialist leader revealed the extent of the changes. Nenni made it clear that, in spite of this neutralist background, the PSI recognized that NATO existed and that Italy was in it; the Socialists did not want to take Italy out of it, but wanted to make sure that the agreements that Italy had signed would be interpreted in a strictly defensive manner.[17] Later in the same month, Nenni asserted that foreign policy was not an important obstacle to PSI collaboration with the Christian Democrats. The greatest difficulties were domestic ones, concerning the structure of the state and society. He pointed out that in other NATO countries there existed forces that, within the framework of continued adherence to the pact, took positions on which the PSI was in perfect agreement; and he referred to the British Labour Party's attitude on atomic neutralization of Germany and the German Social Democrats' attitude on the priority of disarmament over German unification.[18]

In an earlier speech, Nenni had asserted that in principle the Socialists favored the Common Market but just did not trust some of the political forces in power in several Common Market countries.[19] In the spring of 1960, PSI leaders made an exploratory trip to Strasbourg, a headquarters of European community institutions.[20] Nenni and other PSI leaders had never made a secret of the fact that they favored an international *détente*. So did some important private business leaders of Italy, Yugoslav Communists under Tito, and British Conservatives under Macmillan; and so did American Republicans under Eisenhower, at least until the blow-up of the summit conference in May, 1960. The Socialists did not and do not believe that the crucial issue of the political struggle in Italy is participation or nonparticipation in the Atlantic community; in the words of Riccardo Lombardi, "the political struggle revolves about the control of investments." [21]

That the opening to the left, not Italian Communism, was the internal danger against which the Center-Right forces in Italy struggled, and to which foreign policy was to a large extent subordinated, is revealed by that strange behavior of the conservative groups in Italy toward the whole development of an autonomous Socialist Party. The autonomists, led by Nenni, had to struggle not only against the Communists and the left-wing *carristi* within the Socialist ranks, but also against the conservatives, who did everything they could to push the Socialists back into the Communist grasp. The right-wing politicians, churchmen, business leaders, and newspapers lumped Socialists and Communists together and refused to make distinctions. In the 1958 election campaign, the Civic Committees of Catholic Action displayed posters showing two hands manacled together, and under them were the words "A vote for the Socialists is a vote for the Communists." Coalitions between Christian Democrats, Socialists, Social Democrats, and Republicans in local and provincial governments were opposed by clerical intervention or threatened revolt by the right-wing Christian Democrats. In the spring of 1960, similar efforts were under way at the national level when clerical intervention brought them to a halt. The conservatives preferred to push the Socialists into the camp of the revolutionary opposition rather than have them in the camp of constitutional development and reform. They could not really fear the Italian Communist Party, and rightly so, if they chose to push allies toward it.

As a result of the municipal elections of November, 1960, a number of local governments were formed in the following spring based on coalitions among Christian Democrats, Social Democrats, Republicans, and Socialists. They were established in Milan, Genoa, Florence, Venice, and a number of lesser cities in central and northern Italy. Cardinal Siri, chairman of the Vatican's supervisory Committee over Catholic Action, publicly protested this collaboration, appealing to Aldo Moro, the Secretary-General of the Christian Democratic Party, without avail.[22] In the summer of 1961, the Sicilian regional government was reorganized by the Christian Democrats with Socialist support, over the objections of Cardinal Ruffini.

In the autumn of 1961, agitation began once more for an opening to the left at the national level. Again, the whole right-wing sector of Italian politics declared that Socialist support of an Italian government would threaten Italy's commitments to its Atlantic allies. Nenni answered these charges, in Italy and also in the United States, in an article he wrote for *Foreign Affairs*, in January, 1962. He recalled the strong commitment to neutralism in the PSI's history and defended the Socialist vote against NATO in 1949 as consonant with the conditions of the time and a reflection of the domestic politics which, he claimed, provided the real reasons for Italy's entry into the alliance. He continued:

. . . we have never raised the question of withdrawal [from NATO], for two reasons. First, because to do so would convict us of demagoguery; and second, because to withdraw under present conditions would jeopardize the European equilibrium, which though it is dangerously unstable does contribute to the maintenance of a truce between the two opposing blocs.[23]

On January 11, 1962, the PSI central committee adopted a resolution stating that the party did not expect Italy to abandon its alliances but merely insisted that they be given a "purely defensive interpretation." In a report by Riccardo Lombardi, approved by the central committee, "defensive interpretation" was held to mean a refusal to grant atomic weapons to the West German armed forces.[24]

At the end of January, 1962, the Christian Democratic National Party congress, held in Naples, approved a policy calling for a reorganization of the Cabinet to create a new government that would have the parliamentary support of the Socialists. On February 2, 1962, Fanfani submitted his Cabinet's resignation to President Gronchi. Three weeks later a Center-Left coalition Cabinet of Christian Democrats, Social Democrats, and Republicans was formed, predicated on the support of the Socialists for its parliamentary majority. The accompanying program emphasized Italy's continuing loyalty to its Western commitments, gradual nationalization of the electric-power industry, and creation of a committee of ministers with a subordinate committee of experts to plan further economic development.[25] It seemed that the *dirigisti* had won. A major objective of Italian postwar foreign policy apparently had been lost.

At this writing, it is too early to pronounce a definitive judgment. The Socialists and the other left parties may be corrupted into transformism and grant their political support in return for material and honorific rewards rather than for a serious program of planning and reform. This is improbable but not impossible. It is more likely that right-wing Christian Democrats, backed by economic and clerical supporters, will bide their time and later return to the attack, intending to undermine the new program. This happened to the Fanfani Cabinet formed in July, 1958, by Christian Democrats and Social Democrats. At that time, political observers were saying that things in Italy finally would change and real political reform would now take place. Six months later, Fanfani was broken by *francs-tireurs* from the right wing of his party, supported by economic interests and a few conservative cardinals of the Vatican Curia. Awareness that it has happened before, however, should make it less likely to happen again.

FOREIGN GOALS

Although the domestic objective of preserving the existent social structure has predominated in Italian foreign policy, it would be wrong to omit other goals that have also influenced Italy's political leaders. The most important is the restoration of Italy's position in the world, usually described as making Italy's "voice" heard, Italy's *presenza* felt, on the international scene. Numerous examples could be cited, but a few will illustrate the point.

Whenever an Italian government leader meets an important leader of another country, pays a state or informal visit, or attends a conference of an international organization to which not all the other nations in the organization have been invited, all the Italian papers emphasize "the recognition of the importance of Italy's role in international politics at this moment." [26] Italy must be in everything, whatever the price. Italy's application for membership in the United Nations was vetoed five times by the Soviet Union. In spite of this, the Italians supported the Russians' 1955 "package deal" to get Communist states into the United Nations as the price of their own admission. Italy supported another Soviet "package deal" in 1959, creation of the ten-nation disarmament conference at Geneva, so as to be present as one of the five Western states, and thus enabled the Soviet satellites in Eastern Europe to appear also. What contribution was made by Italy or the Soviet satellites is difficult to discover.

Italian governments have consistently opposed any hierarchy within the NATO alliance, constantly emphasizing the equality of all its members.[27] This policy is not the consequence of a passion for the principle of the equality of states in the international system. It is a result of Italy's failure to get into NATO's inner circle. From the beginning, Italy protested against its exclusion from the alliance's military command, originally known as the Directive and Executive Group, later the Permanent Group, which is composed of the United States, Britain, and France.[28] Since then, it has opposed De Gaulle's concept of a Big Three political directorate for the organization. This did not prevent the Italians, however, from proposing a Big Three hierarchy within the European community, which the Benelux countries fear might reduce them to an insignificant role in the Common Market, Euratom, and the Coal and Steel Community.[29]

Italy's efforts to make her presence more noticeable on the world scene extend to aspects of domestic policy. In the summer of 1958, Prime Minister Fanfani proposed a ten-year plan for the development of education and science in Italy. Summing up the various arguments justifying an enormous expenditure in these areas, he concluded:

> With periodic state contributions guaranteed and integrated with those from private sources which will receive tax deductions, the government proposes to encourage scientific research systematically. By this method it will provide for the valorization of the high and free contribution that men of culture give to the development of Italian civilization and to its effective presence in the world.[30]

In the United States, aid to education and science is rationalized in terms of its contribution to national defense; in Italy, in terms of cutting a fine figure in the world.

This preoccupation with making Italy's presence known and voice heard is not confined to left-wing Christian Democrats. Pella of the right wing is as voluble on this subject as Fanfani, and so are the papers and spokesmen of other parties. More sensitive Italians get tired of it. The political critic Francesco Compagna has remarked:

> Pella's policy, obsessed, because of our traditional inferiority complex, with the preoccupation of inserting the "voice of Italy" in the most important international meetings, does not succeed in his intention of making our famous "voice" heard: because as long as it is expressed *ore rotundo* through the present Minister, Italy has really nothing to say.[31]

It is not just a question of the individual minister. It is fundamentally that Italians have no solutions to world problems any more than do experts in the major powers. Italy has a number of highly intelligent and sophisticated analysts of international politics, professional and nonprofessional, but they have come up with no new answers to the problems of a divided Europe, of the Cold War, of armaments, of Asian and African unrest and revolt. Italy does not possess the economic or military strength to make a large contribution to the Atlantic community. It might provide ideas and insights; even perhaps, as some Italian thinkers claim, an effective ideology for the West. Nevertheless, in spite of the intellectual talent undoubtedly present, it has not done so. Perhaps it is too much to claim that "Italy has really nothing to say." It would be more accurate to remark that Italy has not yet said anything original.

Italy's concern with the nation's presence can be explained as typical of a former great power not yet reconciled to its reduced international status. France, especially in De Gaulle's policy of *grandeur*, represents an even more striking and, perhaps, more dangerous example of the same phenomenon. Although Italian politicians have not yet used the word *"grandeur,"* the question remains as to where a policy of *presenza* ends and a policy of *grandezza* begins. In recent Italian history, the pursuit of *grandezza* brought ruin to Italy and sorrow to its neighbors.

I am not satisfied that Italy's reduced international status sufficiently explains the policy of *presenza*. To me, it flows also from deep wellsprings of Italian culture, the concern that all Italians, from the peasant up, have for their fine figure. This concern, transferred to the figure that their nation cuts in the world, reflects the phenomenon of modern nationalism, not rooted deeply in the masses, but present in the political class. Skeptics may dismiss much of the reference to Italy's presence as rhetoric, and many Italians have done so; but politicians and newspapers would not indulge in this particular rhetoric if it evoked no response.

Politicians, diplomats, and intellectuals disagree as to the level of influence to which Italy can properly aspire. Some, such as former President Gronchi, feel that Italy is underrated internationally in the present; treated with "an unjust position of inferiority which also wounds our dignity" [32] Others feel that the revival of Italy's influence is still a matter for the future, and differ as to what form it shall take. Among these there are the aspirants to a renewed role for Italy as a nation state in the world. A young diplomat in the Foreign Office spoke to me in the following terms: "Italy needs twenty years to develop economically and politically; then we shall make our voice heard again in international politics."

Others feel that Italy can have a role in future international affairs only as part of a larger community, Europe; more specifically Western Europe. The myth of a united Europe meant little to the masses, but it has had a response, though variable, within the political class. Some saw in European Union primarily political objectives, others were interested only in possible economic advantages. To some, including both right- and left-wingers, a United Europe bore the possibility of an independent "third force," capable of functioning as an equal of the Soviet and American colossi. The more intelligent of these realized that this goal could be achieved only in a very long run.[33] Others have put aside the "third force" idea and have written of European Union as a means of raising Europe's influence within the Atlantic bloc. For example, Salvatorelli states that Europe will then be "an entity capable of autonomy in respect to the United States. And this autonomy, this independence, will constitute a valid guarantee of peace, against any possible, even if not at all probable, temptation by the major power to abuse the Atlantic instrument." [34]

Since the middle 1950's, however, even the enthusiasts of European political union have recognized the remoteness of this dream. For a while longer they had hopes of achieving at least economic integration. The European Coal and Steel Community appeared to provide the ideal model—a functioning, supernational, integrated organization, with a High Authority not dependent on instructions from or bound by its member states. Those Italians who had more intimate knowledge of the organization soon realized, however, that in practice it was extremely remote from the idealized model. They would concur with the judgment of the American scholar Louis Lister, who has concluded that it bore a far closer resemblance to an intergovernmental agency than to the federal or supernational body that its founders had in mind. It had abolished customs barriers in coal and steel, but it was devoid of political power. In its functioning, the individual governments are strong, the High Authority is weak.[35] This condition was exposed at the time of the coal crisis of 1958–59, when the individual governments placed quotas on coal imports and adopted their own policies to preserve their coal industry, completely excluding the High Authority from any participation in the decisions. The Europeanist Aldo Garosci complained in disgust that the High Authority did not even have the grace to resign in protest.[36]

The treaties constituting the Common Market, Euratom, and the European Investment Bank certainly do not go beyond the Coal and Steel Community in either political or economic integration. Whatever hopes Italian Europeanists had that they might constitute the basis for a new political system in Europe—and these were never very high—were dashed when the Fourth Republic in France was succeeded by the De Gaulle regime. De Gaulle's nationalistic policies of French *grandeur*, his insistence on an independent French atomic military establishment, his unilateral removal of French divisions from NATO command, all pointed up the frustration of the European ideal. When De Gaulle's Premier, Michel Debré, declared that France accepted the organs of "little Europe" as "cooperative agreements," Garosci wrote, "Political Europe is dead by will of the statesmen. . . . For now, all that is offered us is an association among powers for limited ends of *semiliberismo* and of [economic] expansion in third states." [37]

Even before De Gaulle's return to power, it was evident in Italy that serious politicians did not see in "little Europe" a united political force. The best evidence was the caliber of those assigned to the offices of "little Europe" to which the country was entitled. No Italian politician with a future wanted such an appointment. Rome was the place to stay. The Cabinet found it necessary to send either aging politicians, ready for a respectable and honorable retirement position, or else younger men who had abandoned their hopes of political glory at home. At the end of 1957, Giulio Pastore, the longtime leader of the CISL, was scheduled to represent Italy at the headquarters of the Common Market. Because of the prospect of a power struggle inside the CISL over replacing him, the decision was reversed.[38] Pastore remained in Rome; Italian trade-union politics were more important. In 1961, Professor Giuseppe Petrilli was glad to leave the European Investment Bank to return to Rome to head the IRI.

This is not to imply that Italians cannot see benefits or consequences from participation in the Common Market. In the Chamber discussion on ratification of the European treaties, attendance of deputies was very poor.[39] Those few orators who spoke on the treaties discussed them not in terms of a European community but in terms of the effects on Italy.[40] They mentioned prospects for new and expanded foreign markets, for bringing in foreign capital, for forcing rationalization of Italian industry, for more competition and a reduction in prices. They minimized dangers to vested interests.

Many sectors of Italian industry have, since World War II, raised productivity and efficiency so that they are able to compete successfully with the industries of other Common Market countries.[41] Whether they so compete is another question. There is no tradition in Italy, or in any other Continental country, for that matter, that would lead one to believe that the doctrine of free competition has suddenly been wholeheartedly embraced.

In fact, efforts to get effective antitrust legislation in Italy have failed thus far. Elimination of quantitative barriers and reduction of tariffs do not by themselves guarantee competition and lower prices. On goods and services subject to governmental price setting, the record of the Interministerial Committee on Prices has been one of subservience to business and industrial organizations.[42] Italian foreign-exchange restrictions have been subject to past criticisms at meetings of the nations signatory to the General Agreement on Tariffs and Trade.[43] There is evidence of deals between firms of different Common Market countries not to compete, but rather to cooperate in joint marketing arrangements and joint production facilities.[44]

Yet even a casual glance at Italian markets reveals a much larger amount of foreign goods for sale. These come not only from other Common Market countries but from other parts of the world as well. The Common Market, if it has not created a political union, has had a psychological as well as economic effect on the Italian people. Their horizons have been widened. They no longer accept poverty as inevitable. They are less worried about preserving an acquired status or position and more ambitious to achieve a new one. It used to be that every job was considered a tenure job, something to give security for life.[45] Now jobs are not so precious, except for unskilled peasants, because others are available.

Certainly the Common Market deserves some of the credit for this change in atmosphere, as well as for the economic stimulation that has occurred. Even the original Communist Party, in spite of its opposition, has had to admit that the Common Market is forcing the Party to rethink its concepts about the "inevitable decadence of capitalism." [46] Palmiro Togliatti himself has said that the concept of international class struggle no longer makes sense in Western Europe.[47] The Common Market and the Italian boom may force the Communists to openly accept revisionism—a horrible word to the orthodox—as the only policy possible for the Party.

This, perhaps, is projecting events too far and too fast. Old rigidities, local demands for protectionism, for local monopolies, still remain strong.[48] The inflow of foreign goods has not reduced the price level, which, on the contrary, slowly but steadily rises.[49]

A question should be raised as to the justice of crediting the new atmosphere solely to the Common Market. There has been an increase in Italian import and export dealings with many parts of the world. For example, in the first quarter of 1962, Italian exports to other Common Market countries expanded 26.9 per cent over those of the previous year; exports to the United States were up 25 per cent.

Although some look to Europe for political and economic salvation, others turn to the Near East and Africa. Politically, the supporters of this orientation talk about Italy's Mediterranean "vocation" or "mission," defined as "the extension of the sphere of freedom and prosperity in the Mediterranean sector." [50] The political argument runs something like this: For various historic and current reasons, Britain, France, and the United States are suspect and hated by Arabian and African peoples. Italy is not. Italians are *simpatici* and have no racial prejudices. These governments will listen to Italy, whereas they close their ears to the others. Italy has an obligation to contribute to the development of backward areas. Italy can best represent the West in this part of the world, and make Arabs and Africans understand the logic and reasonableness of the West's goals and the benefits they themselves will derive. Italy can be crucial in preventing this vast area from falling under Russian domination.[51]

Opponents and critics look upon this position as nothing more than a rationalization for taking a more independent position and detaching Italy psychologically from its Western allies. Loyalty to the West should come first, they say. They regard this "vocation" as little more than a way of exploiting British and French troubles for Italian political and economic advantage. They question Italy's ability to influence Arab governments effectively. One Italian diplomat said in a personal interview, "Arab politicians can be influenced only by guns and money. Italy has neither to give." He may or may not be right about Arab politicians; he has had long experience with Italian politicians. In any case, Italy has a competitor for this role, for the Germans also have ambitions to become the leading Western power in the Arab world.[52]

The Italian supporters of the Mediterranean "vocation" ignore some inconvenient items. First of all, Italy has a recent colonial and imperialistic past that has not been forgotten, especially in those parts of Africa where it was directly felt. Second, the assumption that Arabs view Italy differently from other Western nations is highly questionable. At least one Arab, Charles Issawi, has asserted that the Arab world does not look upon the West as discrete parts but tends to picture it as an entity, toward which the Arab attitude is negative and hostile.[53]

Any assertion of a Mediterranean "mission" immediately calls to mind Mussolini brandishing the sword of Islam. The strange fact is, however, that many of the parties associated with the idea in recent years are on the left side of the spectrum, while the Fascists have been among the most orthodox of Atlanticists, whatever their private opinions of their allies. The explanation appears to be that we have here a rhetorical cover for Enrico Mattei's oil operations in the Middle East and North Africa, and the parties and factions of the Christian Democratic Party that benefited from his major support found ways of justifying his operations to the nations of his foreign competitors and to Italian public opinion.*

If this were all one could find in the Mediterranean "vocation," there need be little worry. Italian businessmen, whether from the public or private sector of the economy, have as much right to do

---

* On September 12, 1960, Mattei, speaking at a conference in Piacenza, attacked the existing structure of the world oil industry. He said a new set of agreements was needed, based not on the interests of the oil companies but on the interests of the producing countries and the consuming public. He added that Italy had given an example of such a policy. He attributed the decline of oil prices to a fundamental crisis. "The crisis derives substantially from two facts: the rise in the number of operators and the growing intervention of governments in oil questions to protect consumers against the greed of the companies." *New York Times,* September 13, 1960.

The Goals

151

business in those parts of the world as German, British, French, American, Soviet, and other businessmen. The danger stems from the necessity to give a political and rhetorical rationale to such operations. The tradition of the "mission" is too close to the surface, too recent, too associated with grand gestures, merely to be shrugged off as an example of irresponsible language. The world has already paid a high price for irresponsible language.

Although Italians complain constantly of a chronic shortage of capital, a considerable portion of the available capital appears to go to areas other than Italy. Much of Italy itself is underdeveloped, and it would appear that Italy's highest "mission" lies right at home. Some contend that the Italian south is as about as developed as it can be, given its fundamental resource deficiencies, and that it is better to invest in Africa or wherever else there are resources that can be developed and money made. This argument abandons the Italian poor to a future without hope, for even if the foreign investments are profitable and properly taxed, the most the poor could get from them is more relief, not a solution. This does not suggest that the ENI should throw away money in southern Italy to find oil if none is there.* An anonymous editorialist in the Turin newspaper *La Stampa* drove the point home:

Perhaps the most valid contribution to Atlantic security that we can make is to elevate our own depressed areas. Italy, of all the Western allies, has the largest number of unemployed and illiterates: an excellent incentive to Communist Party propaganda, which in the last years has not declined in strength. . . . Before giving prosperity and freedom to colonial peoples, we must assure them in our own house. Grand gestures in foreign policy have always been diversions, sought by nationalist governments in order not to impose on the privileged classes the necessary sacrifices to defeat poverty.[54]

The conclusion is a partial truth. The grand gestures have also been sought for their own sake.

A favorite gesture is playing the role of mediator. This has an almost obsessive appeal. When French planes bombed a Tunisian

* Offshore oil has been found at Gela, Sicily. Gulf Oil Company also has found oil in Sicily.

town near the Algerian frontier in March, 1958, Foreign Minister Pella, on the basis of an erroneous newspaper report, publicly announced his readiness to mediate the incident. To his chagrin, he learned that the French wanted no intervention, and thereby suffered a loss of face at home.

This is, of course, a minor incident. Far more serious is the enchantment with the idea that Italy could play the role of mediator between the superpowers. Sforza had such a vision in the years immediately after World War II. Even when accepting Marshall Plan aid, he assured the Constituent Assembly that "Italy is not blindly aligned behind anyone." [55] Prime Minister De Gasperi backed him up, affirming that "we are not taking part, in any form, in any measure, in eventual attempts—assuming they may be made—to isolate Russia, or in attempts that could lead to later blocs." [56] Later Sforza thought of joining with France, which had similar ambitions in that period, to play together the role of mediator or "third force." [57] By the autumn of 1948, Sforza had abandoned the idea, and on October 13 he told Secretary of State Marshall that "neutrality was by now a vain formula and that we were all out with the United States." [58]

Sforza and De Gasperi may have swung over to the American camp, but the idea that Italy could influence Russia on behalf of the West did not die. As late as the spring of 1960, President Gronchi, on his visit to Moscow, had hopes of playing a reconciling if not mediating role between the two colossi.

This image of Italy as a conciliator or mediator has been severely criticized by Gaetano Martino, who says it is incompatible with Italy's membership in the Atlantic alliance. If Italy wants to reconcile divergent points of view between European and Arab countries, or between the United States and the Soviet Union, Martino argues, Italy cannot be on either side, but must be outside both camps. To be a mediator, Italy must abandon its Western commitment.[59]

The argument is too logical to square with political realities; abandonment is not at all necessary. Martino was merely indulging in a political attack on Fanfani and Saragat, both supporters of the Mediterranean "vocation." Macmillan of Britain has engaged in similar efforts vis-à-vis the United States and Russia, without any greater success but without abandoning Britain's crucial position in NATO.

Why do the Italians persist in their efforts, often at nobody's behest, to play the role of conciliator? One reasonable answer is that they, like the British and others, are terrified of a clash that would destroy all Europe. (The bitter slogan in England is "No annihilation without representation.") Another reason is the Italian foreign-policy tradition of taking a walk, getting into an uncommitted position as the best bargaining point to acquire small gains—the tradition of *sacro egoismo*.

I believe that the explanation must go beyond foreign-policy considerations or traditions, however, and must also take into account the social and political culture. Playing mediator is one way of getting others to take notice of Italy, to make the famous "voice" heard in the world. We should further consider the domestic "transformist" tradition, the penchant for making a deal that compromises the most incompatible political positions. The feeling that "black, white, red, they are all alike," which has such deep roots in Italian society, carries over to the international level. It results in a tendency to look for an easy solution to cover up a conflict of interest, rather than to face up to the conflict. For if one is not ideological or moralistic about an issue, the equitable price can be found.

The cynical motivations behind some of the most moral positions can be illustrated by the preoccupation with internal political considerations, especially party-electoral or personal ambitions. Two examples follow: The whole Trieste problem, an issue that generated true emotion, was handled, in terms of timing, negotiations, and positions taken, primarily with electoral considerations in mind. In June, 1958, the Hungarian Government executed Nagy and Meleter after one and a half years of imprisonment. The large Italian newspapers printed violent denunciations and protests. Foreign Minister Pella bitterly condemned the moral outrage in Parliament and recalled the Italian Ambassador from Budapest in protest, a gesture made by no other country. An inquiry into the reasons for these outbursts revealed that with a new government in the process of being formed by Fanfani, the large papers backing the Liberal Party were trying to get the party into the government, and Pella was trying to hold onto the Foreign Ministry for himself. Neither succeeded. Fanfani formed a coalition with the Social Democrats and took over both the Prime Ministry and Foreign Ministry.

The amount of emotion expressed on a political subject appears, curiously, in inverse proportion to the degree of emotion actually felt. Contemporary Italy presents a picture of political apathy and indifference. A common attitude to the government and the state is that they are a bother and a nuisance; people wish they would go away and leave them alone to go about their business.* This atmosphere raises again the problem of neutralism, inherent in the discussion on Italy as a self-appointed mediator. Only one party, the Communist, is officially committed to neutralism today. Undoubtedly there are Socialist factions and others, including Catholics, who would prefer Italy to be neutral. Only in the most unlikely event of a Communist take-over, however, would the country be openly brought into the neutralist camp.†

The Italians' tendency toward neutralism is not positive or well thought out. Rather, it is negative, a product of indifference, ignorance, or lack of commitment, and it is difficult to conceive of a vital and dynamic public opinion responding to a great crisis.

This does not mean, of course, that an Italian Government would not live up to its commitments if Soviet forces attacked in Europe. Salandra did not in 1914, and Mussolini did not in 1939, but both could adduce good legal reasons why the *casus foederis* was not applicable to Italy at those times. It means that large numbers of the

---

* We see here the persistence of an historic attitude toward political authority, summed up in the following sentence of Leonardo Olschki: "In the public opinion of Italy the government—*il governo*—still remained an institution detached from the people, who continued to consider the executive authorities as exploiters and the laws as an imposition and duress" (*The Genius of Italy*, p. 451). Some commentators claim to see a recent revival of political interest within Italy, especially among younger age groups, since the riots of the summer of 1960 which led to the downfall of the Tambroni Government. See Adolfo Battaglia, "La strettoia," *Il Mondo*, February 21, 1961, p. 1.

† The Communist Party has stated that if it should come to power it would not bring Italy into the Soviet bloc but would adopt a position of neutrality. This statement can, of course, be treated with skepticism, but there are geographical and economic reasons why the Communists might adopt formal neutrality. The United States Navy controls the Mediterranean Sea. It would, in any case, be a pro-Soviet neutrality. There is evidence, however, that large masses of Communist voters are not anti-American and some analysts argue that a sizable segment of the leadership is not anti-American. If this segment of the leadership, called the "Italians," could wrest control of the party from the "Russians" (Togliatti, Longo, etc., who spent years in Moscow), the Party might adopt a real neutralist position, as does Yugoslavia. The evidence for such a possibility is meager, and the Togliatti-Longo group appears to be firmly in control.

Italian people might not live up to the government's commitments. We can hope that this will continue to remain speculative and that neither the government nor the people will be put to the test.

In Italy, as elsewhere, a very few will decide. Who they will be in Italy is difficult to tell. For a long time now, formal authority has not been effective authority. Since De Gasperi's days, power has become shifting and diffuse. Sometimes it seems to be located in the Prime Minister and the Cabinet, at other times in the secretaries-general and executive bureaus of the parties, and at still other times, apparently, nowhere. If, in retrospect, De Gasperi appears to have been a tower of strength and authority, this vision of him is probably exaggerated, for there is abundant evidence of his shifts and retreats under pressures. But at least it was possible to identify who was shifting and retreating. Fanfani is the only Christian Democrat since 1953 who has attempted to build up a commanding political position, but up to now he has failed. Too many interests and individuals have a stake in keeping a weak executive—economic, clerical, factional, and personal interests. Under such circumstances both foreign policy and domestic policy drift; a move in one direction is immediately countered by a move in the other.

Under such circumstances, strong direction and, perhaps, domination, from the outside has a minimum of justification. It is only a minimum, however, for natural, justifiable pride and integrity cannot endure such a situation indefinitely. There are many Italians with pride and integrity who recognize that Italy's major contribution to the peace of the world and the security of the West will be to overcome its internal political and economic contradictions and put its house in order. The capacity to do this, however, requires eliminating the underlying lack of consensus, which appears to be the root of Italy's difficulties. As long as Italian society remains "fractured," as long as substantial proportions of the population remain "outside the state," the strongest political leader can do little substantial in pursuing consistent foreign policies that require real support. Personal sacrifice or a high economic cost cannot be demanded from a people who have no stake in their own social and political institutions. With the best of intentions and greatest of capacities, overcoming these handicaps requires time, measured perhaps in decades if not generations.

Most of the other states of the world resemble Italy in this fundamental characteristic of an underlying absence of the consensus needed to bolster the social and political order. This study has been concerned with analyzing political processes specifically, and many of the described characteristics are obviously not unique. Comparative analyses of the politics of foreign policy-making in other "fractured" political systems might highlight which characteristics are common to many and which are peculiar to a given society. It is hoped that the present study may make a contribution to an expansion of knowledge in this area.

Notes

NOTES

CHAPTER 1: Social and Political Attitudes

1. Edward C. Banfield, *The Moral Basis of a Backward Society* (Glencoe, Ill.: The Free Press of Glencoe, 1958), p. 85.
2. *Ibid.*, p. 116.
3. *Ibid.*, pp. 65–66.
4. *Ibid.*, p. 124.
5. Sebastiano Aglianò, *Questa Sicilia* (Milan: Mondadori, 1950), pp. 39, 62–65, 76.
6. Jean-François Revel, *Pour l'Italie* (Paris: René Julliard, 1958), p. 173. See also Ignazio Silone, "A Courageous Priest. A Note on Don Lorenzo Milani," *Texas Quarterly*, Summer, 1961, p. 200.
7. Quoted in Hadley Cantril, *Faith, Hope and Heresy: The Psychology of the Protest Voter* (Princeton, N.J.: Institute for International Social Research, 1958), p. 46.
8. Elena Croce, "On Being Italian," *Texas Quarterly*, Summer, 1961, pp. 40–48. See also Carlo Sforza, *Italy and the Italians* (London: Frederick Muller, 1948), p. 90.
9. Joseph Justman, *The Italian People and Their Schools* (Tiffin, Ohio: Kappa Delta Pi, 1958), p. 5.
10. Giuseppe Borgese, *Goliath: The March of Fascism* (New York: Viking Press, 1937), p. 88.
11. Revel, *Pour l'Italie*, p. 171.
12. Borgese, *Goliath*, p. 88.
13. II. Stuart Hughes, *Consciousness and Society* (New York: Alfred A. Knopf, 1958), p. 201.
14. Luigi Sturzo, *Italy and Fascismo* (New York: Harcourt, Brace, 1926), pp. 66–67.
15. Banfield, *The Moral Basis of a Backward Society*, pp. 85, 87, 91, 98, 99, 102.
16. Giacomo Perticone, *La formazione della classe politica nell' Italia contemporanea* (Florence: Sansoni, 1954), pp. 87–88.
17. *Ibid.*, p. 174.
18. See Joseph LaPalombara, "Political Party Systems and Crisis Government: French and Italian Contrasts," *Midwest Journal of Political Science*, May, 1958, p. 131.
19. George Kish, "Fattori generali dei comportamenti elettorali in Italia," *Nord e Sud*, January, 1958, p. 87. It is obvious that Italy is far from unique in respect to these influences on voting behavior.

20. Leopoldo Piccardi, *La storia non aspetta* (Bari: Laterza, 1957), p. 29.
21. Revel, *Pour l'Italie*, p. 88.
22. Otto Kirchheimer, "Majorities and Minorities in Western European Governments," *Western Political Quarterly*, June, 1959, pp. 506–7.
23. Giovanni Gronchi, *Discorsi d'America* (Milan: Garzanti, 1956), p. 99.
24. *Ibid.*, p. 39.
25. *La formazione*, p. xii.
26. Pierpaolo Luzzatto Fegiz, *Il volto sconosciuto dell' Italia* (Milan: Giuffre, 1956), pp. 487–88.
27. Perticone, *La formazione*, pp. 175–76, 181.
28. *Ibid.*, pp. xv–xvi.
29. *Ibid.*, p. 156.
30. Gaetano Salvemini, *Clericali e laici* (Florence: Parenti, 1957), pp. 85–86.
31. Paolo Pavolini, "I sette socialismi," *Il Mondo* (Rome), August 26, 1958, p. 3.
32. Perticone, *La formazione*, p. 266.
33. *Italy and the Italians*, p. 85.
34. Guido Piovene, "An Ideal Journey Through Italy," *Perspective of Italy* (An *Atlantic Monthly* supplement), 1958, p. 13.
35. Clifford A. L. Rich, "The Growth of Political Institutions in the Italian Republic" (Unpublished Ph.D. dissertation, University of California at Berkeley, 1950), pp. 359–60.
36. In Dante Benedetti, *De Gasperi politico e statista* (Rome: G.D.M., 1949), pp. xxiii–xxxiii.
37. Giuseppe Maranini, *Miti e realtà della democrazia* (Milan: Communità, 1958), p. 94. Maranini claims credit for invention of the word "*partitocrazia*."
38. Ignazio Silone, "Gli apparati e la democrazia," *Tempo presente*, May, 1957, p. 363.
39. Vittorio de Caprariis, "Problemi istituzionali della democrazia moderna," *Nord e Sud*, June, 1959, p. 16.
40. *Ibid.*, p. 24.
41. *Goliath*, p. 144.

CHAPTER 2: The Political Audience—Composition and Stereotypes

1. Istituto italiano dell' opinione pubblica, "Le principali fonti d'informazione degli Italiani in politica," *L'opinione*, April–May, 1958, p. 17.
2. Enzo Forcella, "Millecinquecento lettori," *Tempo presente*, June, 1959, p. 451.
3. *The United States Public and the United Nations* (New York: Carnegie Endowment for International Peace, 1958), pp. 10, 16.
4. Luzzatto Fegiz, *Il volto sconosciuto*, pp. 339–40.
5. *Ibid.*, pp. 518–19.
6. *Ibid.*, pp. 412, 438.
7. Pavolini, "I sette socialismi," *Il Mondo*, August 26, 1958, p. 3. See also Alessandro Pizzorno, "The Italian Socialist Party and Political Participation," *Production, Research, Organization, and Design Translations*, December, 1959, pp. 25–31.

8. Quoted in Alberto Tarchiani, *Dieci anni tra Roma e Washington* (Milan: Mondadori, 1955), p. 203 n.

9. Carlo Sforza, *Cinque anni a Palazzo chigi* (Rome: Atlante, 1952), p. 99.

10. Unpublished manuscript, p. 35.

11. René Albrecht-Carrié, *Italy from Napoleon to Mussolini* (New York: Columbia University Press, 1950), p. 4.

12. The phrases within quotation marks have been extracted from the annual report for 1957 to the Foreign Affairs Committee of the Chamber of Deputies by its Secretary, Professor Giuseppe Vedovato. See the report in *Rivista di studi politici internazionali*, January–March, 1958, pp. 87–118.

13. Luzzatto Fegiz, *Il volto sconosciuto*, p. 709.

14. *Ibid.*, pp. 728–29.

15. *Ibid.*, p. 729.

16. *Ibid.*, p. 710.

17. "Auspex," "La situazione attuale nel medio oriente," *Rivista di studi politici internazionali*, April–June, 1957, p. 214.

18. *Il Mondo*, June 9, 1959, p. 2.

19. Luzzatto Fegiz, *Il volto sconosciuto*, p. 675.

20. *Ibid.*, pp. 712–13.

CHAPTER 3: Historic Ends and Means in Italian Foreign Policy

1. *Goliath*, p. 114.

2. Federico Chabod, "Considerazioni sulla politica estera dell' Italia dal 1870 al 1915," in *Orientamenti per la storia d'Italia nel Risorgimento* (Bari: Laterza, 1952), pp. 19–23. See also Chabod, *Storia della politica estera italiana dal 1870 al 1896, Le premesse*, Vol. I (Bari: Laterza, 1951).

3. Renato Giordano, *Il mercato commune e i suoi problemi* (Rome: Opere Nuove, 1958), pp. 9–10.

4. Chabod, "Considerazioni sulla politica estera," pp. 27–28, 35.

5. Dennis Mack Smith, *Italy: A Modern History* (Ann Arbor, Mich.: University of Michigan Press, 1959), p. 145.

6. Dante L. Germino, *The Italian Fascist Party in Power* (Minneapolis, Minn.: University of Minnesota Press, 1959), p. 11.

7. William C. Askew, "The Austro-Italian Antagonism, 1896–1914," in *Power, Public Opinion, and Diplomacy*, Lillian Parker Wallace and William C. Askew (eds.) (Durham, N.C.: Duke University Press, 1959), pp. 173–74.

8. Mack Smith, *Italy*, p. 28.

9. *Ibid.*, pp. 120, 218.

10. Askew, "The Austro-Italian Antagonism, 1896–1914," pp. 182–83.

11. Mack Smith, *Italy*, p. 20.

12. Albrecht-Carrié, *Italy from Napoleon to Mussolini*, pp. 74–75.

13. Quoted in H. Stuart Hughes, "The Early Diplomacy of Italian Fascism: 1922–1932," in *The Diplomats: 1919–1939*, Gordon A. Craig and Felix Gilbert (eds.) (Princeton, N.J.: Princeton University Press, 1953), p. 210.

14. William C. Askew, *Europe and Italy's Acquisition of Libya, 1911–12* (Durham, N.C.: Duke University Press, 1942).

15. Quoted in Felix Gilbert, "Ciano and His Ambassadors," in *The Diplomats*, Craig and Gilbert (eds.), p. 513.

16. Albrecht-Carrié, *Italy from Napoleon to Mussolini*, pp. 56, 64.
17. Enzo Tagliacozzo, *Gaetano Salvemini nel cinquantennio liberale* (Florence: La Nuova Italia, 1959), p. 150.
18. Mack Smith, *Italy*, p. 28.
19. Tagliacozzo, *Gaetano Salvemini*, p. 150.
20. Mack Smith, *Italy*, pp. 296–307.
21. *Ibid.*, p. 304.
22. Benedetti, *De Gasperi*, p. 92.
23. Speech of December 23, 1940; in *New York Times*, December 24, 1940.
24. Arturo Carlo Jemolo, *Chiesa e stato in Italia negli ultimi cento anni* (Turin: Einaudi, 1952), pp. 671–73.
25. *L'Italia nella seconda guerra mondiale* (Milan: Mondadori, 1946), pp. 37–39.
26. Hughes, "The Early Diplomacy of Italian Fascism, 1922–1932," p. 215.
27. *Ibid.*, p. 226.
28. *Ibid.*, p. 217.
29. *Ibid.*, p. 231.
30. Gilbert, "Ciano and His Ambassadors," p. 513.
31. *Ibid.*, p. 526.
32. *Ibid.*, pp. 517–20.
33. *Ibid.*, p. 516.
34. *Ibid.*, pp. 530–36.
35. Askew, "The Austro-Italian Antagonism, 1896–1914," p. 175.
36. Tagliacozzo, *Gaetano Salvemini*, pp. 157–74.
37. *Discorsi d'America*, p. 17.
38. Italy, Camera dei deputati, *Atti parlamentari*, 3rd Leg., Vols. 1958, pp. 73–75.
39. Maranini, *Miti e realtà della democrazia*, p. 235.
40. From a speech by former Foreign Minister Giuseppe Pella to the Senate on October 24, 1957. Italy, Senato della Repubblica, *Atti parlamentari*, 2nd Leg., Vols. 1957, pp. 24559–69.
41. *Discorsi*, p. 88.
42. *Il Popolo* (Rome), May 9, 1958.
43. "Auspex," "La situazione attuale nel medio oriente," p. 227.
44. Gaetano Martino, *L'idea liberale nella politica estera italiana* (Rome: Partito liberale italiano, 1958), pp. 3–4.
45. Massimo Magistrati, "Dieci anni di cooperazione internazionale," *Rivista di studi politici internazionali*, January–March, 1958, p. 10.
46. Mario Toscano, "The Balance of Impotence," *Hopkins Bologna Center Review*, Fall, 1958–Winter, 1959, p. 9.
47. *Ibid.*, pp. 26–27. A similar point is made by historian Luigi Salvatorelli, *La guerra fredda (1945–1955)* (Venice: Neri Pozza, 1956), p. 105.
48. Giordano, *Il mercato commune*, pp. 12–14.
49. Oronzo Reale, *Lotta su due fronti* (Rome: Partito repubblicano italiano, 1958), p. 8.
50. Gilbert, "Ciano and His Ambassadors," p. 525.
51. Sforza, *Cinque anni a Palazzo chigi*, p. 183.
52. *Ibid.*, pp. 183–84.
53. Sforza, *Italy and the Italians*, p. 122.
54. A report on this conference was printed in *Il Crociato*, October 31, 1959.
55. Gronchi, *Discorsi d'America*, p. 83.

CHAPTER 4: The Party Organizations

1. Silone, "Gli apparati e la democrazia," p. 363; Maranini, *Miti e realtà della democrazia*, pp. 23, 94.
2. Giovanni Malagodi, "Il segretario e gli 'apparati,'" *Tempo presente*, February, 1959, pp. 137–41.
3. Marco Cesarini Sforza, "Il regionalismo dei democratici," *Nord e Sud*, March, 1960, p. 21.
4. *U.S. News & World Report*, May 30, 1960, pp. 73–74.
5. Murray Edelman, "Sources of Popular Support for the Italian Christian Democratic Party in the Postwar Decade," *Midwest Journal of Political Science*, May, 1958, pp. 143–59.
6. In 1956, Free and Sereno took an opposite point of view. See *Italy: Dependent Ally or Independent Partner?*, pp. 95–108.
7. Muriel Grindrod, *The Rebuilding of Italy* (London: Royal Institute of International Affairs, 1955), pp. 75–81.
8. Gilbert, "Ciano and His Ambassadors," p. 518.
9. For a brief history in English of the party, see W. Hilton-Young, *The Italian Left, A Short History of Political Socialism in Italy* (London: Longmans, Green and Co. Ltd., 1959); also Richard Hostetter, *The Italian Socialist Movement*, Vol. I (Princeton, N.J: D. Van Nostrand, 1958).
10. Pietro Nenni, "Che cosa vuole il Partito socialista?" *Una battaglia vinta* (Rome: Leonardo, 1946), p. 18.
11. *Avanti* (Rome), July 2, 1958.
12. Giuseppe Galasso, "P.C.I. 1960," *Nord e Sud*, May, 1960, p. 21.
13. Official figures of the Ministry of the Interior as published in *La Stampa* (Turin), June 6, 1958.
14. Speech by Togliatti to the Central Committee, *L'Unità*, September 29, 1957. See also Norman Kogan, "National Communism vs. the National Way to Communism—An Italian Interpretation," *Western Political Quarterly*, September, 1958, pp. 660–72.
15. *L'Unità*, October 1, 1957.
16. Galasso, "P.C.I. 1960," p. 17.
17. *Ibid.*, p. 21.
18. *Ibid.*, p. 23.
19. Tarchiani, *Dieci anni tra Roma e Washington*, pp. 151–52.
20. Kirchheimer, "Majorities and Minorities in Western European Governments," pp. 506–7.
21. Pietro Quaroni, *Valigia diplomatica* (Milan: Garzanti, 1956), p. 141.
22. Tarchiani, *Dieci anni tra Roma e Washington*, p. 138.

CHAPTER 5: The Parliament, the Cabinet, and the President

1. Speech by Cesare Merzagora, President of the Senate. The full text is reprinted in Armando Saitta, *Storia e miti del '900* (Bari: Laterza, 1960), pp. 938–41.
2. Perticone, *La formazione*, pp. 192–95.
3. *Relazioni Internazionali*, August 10–17, 1957, pp. 963.

4. Maranini, *Miti e realtà della democrazia*, p. 229.
5. See *Il Messagero* (Rome), January 16, 17, 18, 1958.
6. "Adstans" [Paolo Canali], *Alcide De Gasperi nella politica estera italiana (1944–1953)* (Milan: Mondadori, 1953), pp. 70–71. Canali was head of De Gasperi's foreign-affairs section.
7. Sforza, *Cinque anni a Palazzo chigi*, p. 8.
8. Hughes, "The Early Diplomacy of Italian Fascism, 1922–1932," p. 217.
9. *Ibid.*, p. 218.
10. Mack Smith, *Italy*, p. 281.
11. An English translation of the Constitution of the Italian Republic can be found in Italy, Presidency of the Council of Ministers, *Ten Years of Italian Democracy 1946–1956* (Rome: Presidency of the Council of Ministers, 1956), pp. 5–35.
12. *Il Popolo*, November 1, 1957.
13. *New York Times*, April 8, 1960.

CHAPTER 6: The Church

1. Editorial, May 17, 1960; a full English translation appears in *U.S. News & World Report*, May 30, 1960, pp. 73–74.
2. Editorial by Cardinal Ottaviani in the official organ of the Italian Catholic Action Society, *Il Quotidiano*, January 21, 1958.
3. *La Stampa*, January 8, 1958.
4. *Ibid.*
5. Text in Saitta, *Storia e miti del '900*, pp. 938–41.
6. The complete text was published in *L'Osservatore romano*, May 4, 1958.
7. On the historical background, see the substantial work of Arturo Carlo Jemolo, *Chiesa e stato in Italia negli ultimi cento anni.*
8. Ferruccio Parri, "I poteri del presidente," *Il Ponte*, July, 1957, p. 995.
9. Joseph LaPalombara, "The Utility and Limitations of Interest Group Theory in Non-American Field Situations," *Journal of Politics*, February, 1960, p. 41.
10. Carlo Falconi, *La Chiesa e le organizzazioni cattoliche in Italia* (Turin: Einaudi, 1956), p. 426. Part V of this book is concerned with Church intervention in Italian domestic affairs.
11. Carlo Falconi, *Il pentagono vaticano* (Bari: Laterza, 1958), pp. 156–57.
12. *Ibid.*, p. 168.
13. *U.S. News & World Report*, May 30, 1960, p. 73.
14. Quoted in Ernesto Buonaiuti, *La Chiesa e il Communismo* (Rome: Bompiani, 1945), p. 13.
15. Robert J. Graham, S.J., *Vatican Diplomacy* (Princeton, N.J.: Princeton University Press, 1959), p. 352.
16. Falconi, *La Chiesa e le organizzazioni cattoliche in Italia*, pp. 595–98.
17. Tarchiani, *Dieci anni tra Roma e Washington*, pp. 156–57.
18. Sforza, *Cinque anni a Palazzo chigi*, p. 207.
19. Falconi, *La Chiesa e le organizzazioni cattoliche in Italia*, pp. 593, 597–98, 624.
20. *Il Pentagono vaticano*, pp. 179–88.

21. *Il Crociato*, August 1, 1959.
22. *Il Pentagono vaticano*, pp. 179–88. See also Furio Monicelli, "Il gesuita contemporaneo," *Il Mondo*, January 26, 1960, pp. 3–4.
23. *New York Times*, January 8, 1960.
24. Ernesto Rossi, "La ragione pratica," *Il Mondo*, May 3, 1960, pp. 1–2.
25. *Vatican Diplomacy*, p. 352.
26. Extracts from this letter were published in *Il Crociato*, June 18, 1960. The reports in *L'Osservatore romano* and *Il Quotidiano* distorted the sense and tone of Cardinal Montini's letter. See *Il Mondo*, June 14, 1960, p. 2.
27. *L'Osservatore romano*, December 13, 1961.

CHAPTER 7: Other Pressure Groups

1. Roberto Ducci, "Preistoria dell' unificazione europea," *Nuova Antologia*, March, 1960, pp. 292, 308.
2. Quoted in *Il Mondo*, April 5, 1960, p. 2.
3. The above description of the business and financial community was furnished to me by a Milan banker. See also Mario Einaudi, *et al.*, *Nationalization in France and Italy* (Ithaca, N.Y.: Cornell University Press, 1955), pp. 18–58, 191–246.
4. Adam Abruzzi, "Labor Supply and Productivity in Italy," *Reprint of Speeches on Italy Delivered at the Orientation Seminar on "Setting Up Operations Under the Common Market"* (New York: American Management Association, 1958), pp. 61–62.
5. LaPalombara, "The Utility and Limitations of Interest Group Theory in Non-American Field Situations," pp. 143–44. See also Joseph LaPalombara, "La Confindustria e la politica in Italia," *Tempi moderni*, October–December, 1961, pp. 3–16.
6. Quoted in *Il Mondo*, December 29, 1959, p. 2, and May 17, 1960, p. 2.
7. LaPalombara, "The Utility and Limitations of Interest Group Theory in Non-American Field Situations," pp. 44–45.
8. Quoted by Ernesto Rossi, "Le bugie del barone," *Il Mondo*, March 29, 1960, p. 2.
9. Falconi, *Il Pentagono vaticano*, pp. 83–95.
10. *New York Times*, November 23, 29, 1959.
11. Sforza, *Cinque anni a Palazzo chigi*, p. 108.
12. Massimo Magistrati, "Da Messina al Campidoglio," *Rivista di studi politici internazionali*, April–June, 1957, p. 196.
13. Letter of the Vice Director-General of Economic Affairs in the Foreign Ministry, Roberto Ducci, in *Il Mondo*, August 20, 1957, p. 6.
14. *La Stampa*, February 27, 28, March 12, 1958.
15. Reported by Aldo Garosci, "Ventesimo secolo," *Il Mondo*, January 20, 1959, p. 4, and July 14, 1959, p. 4.
16. For an interesting coincidence that occurred at the end of June, 1958, see *Il Tempo* (Rome), July 1, 1958.
17. See, for example, a speech by Count Carlo Sforza in the Chamber of Deputies, March, 1948. Sforza, *Cinque anni a Palazzo chigi*, p. 223.

18. Italian Information Office, *Italian Report,* July, 1962, pp. 19–22.
19. *La Stampa,* December 4, 1957.
20. B. C., "I rapporti italo-jugoslavi," *Relazioni internazionali,* June 21, 1958, pp. 707–8.
21. Paolo N. Rogers, "La diplomazia nel mondo economico attuale," *Hopkins Bologna Review,* Fall-Winter, 1959–1960, p. 12.
22. Magliano, *La borghesia e la paura,* pp. 151–52.
23. Andrew and Jane Carey, "Oil for the Lamps of Italy," *Political Science Quarterly,* June, 1958, pp. 234–253; Claire Sterling, "Mattei the Condottiere," *The Reporter,* March 20, 1958, pp. 20–23.
24. *New York Times,* June 14, 1960.
25. *Il Giorno* (Milan), May 6, 1958.
26. Joseph LaPalombara, *The Italian Labor Movement: Problems and Prospects* (Ithaca, N.Y.: Cornell University Press, 1957), pp. 71–104. See also Maurice F. Neufeld, *Italy, School for Awakening Countries* (Ithaca, N.Y.: Cornell University Press, 1961).
27. Abruzzi, "Labor Supply and Productivity in Italy," p. 59.
28. LaPalombara, *The Italian Labor Movement,* p. 56.
29. *Ibid.,* p. 180.
30. *Ibid.,* p. 121.
31. *Il Mondo,* February 9, 1960, pp. 3–4.
32. *Ibid.,* November 24, 1959, p. 2.
33. *Ibid.,* January 19, 1960, p. 4.
34. *Ibid.,* April 26, 1960, p. 4.
35. LaPalombara, *The Italian Labor Movement,* p. 57.
36. Lewis L. Lorwin, *The International Labor Movement* (New York: Harper & Brothers, 1953), p. 328.
37. See Giuseppe Ciranna, "Un 'gruppo di pressione': La Confederazione Nazionale Coltivatori Diretti," *Nord e Sud,* January, 1958, pp. 9–39.
38. LaPalombara, "The Utility and Limitations of Interest Group Theory in Non-American Field Situations," p. 40.
39. *New York Times,* November 27, 1959.
40. *Ibid.,* February 4, 1962.
41. *Il Messagero,* May 20, 1957.
42. Leonardo Olschki, *The Genius of Italy* (New York: Oxford University Press, 1949), pp. 452–54.

CHAPTER 8: The Bureaucracy

1. Italy, Ministero degli Affari Esteri, *Elenchi del personale* (Rome: Tipografia riservata del Ministero degli Affari Esteri, 1958), pp. 7–10.
2. For a complete description of requirements for taking the examination and for passing it, see Italy, Ministero degli Affari Esteri, *Concorso per esami a 16 posti di volontario nella carriera diplomatico consolare,* Estratto dalla *Gazzetta Ufficiale,* December 19, 1957, n. 314.
3. See L. V. Ferraris, *L'amministrazione centrale del Ministero degli esteri italiano nel suo sviluppo storico 1848–1954* (Florence: Biblioteca della "Rivista di studi politici internazionali," 1955).
4. Perticone, *La formazione,* pp. 204–5.

5. The argument is recounted in Tarchiani, *Dieci anni tra Roma e Washington*, pp. 240–70.

6. See Chapter 2, p. 23.

7. Nicolò Carandini, "Purga a Palazzo chigi," *Il Mondo*, November 25, 1958, p. 1. For an attack on factionalism inside the Foreign Office, see Gian Giacomo Bassano, "I migliori anni di Palazzo chigi," *Nuova Antologia*, February, 1961, pp. 207–18.

8. Letter to the editor of *Il Mondo*, December 24, 1957, p. 12.

9. As one example, see Burton Sapin, Richard C. Snyder, and H. W. Bruck, *An Appropriate Role for the Military in American Foreign Policy-making: A Research Note* (Princeton, N.J.: Organizational Behavior Section, Princeton University, 1954).

10. Quotation and statistics from Giorgio Moscon, "L'esercito non è un cantiere per disoccupati," *Il Ponte*, February, 1960, pp. 146–48.

11. Paolo Pavolini, "Cinquemila miliardi," *Il Mondo*, February 24, 1959, p. 3.

12. For a more detailed description of the status of the Italian armed forces, see J. Wullus-Rudiger, "Italy's Role Within NATO," *Military Review*, February, 1959, p. 103.

13. Mack Smith, *Italy*, p. 28.

14. Rogers, "La diplomazia nel mondo economico attuale," p. 11.

CHAPTER 9: External Forces

1. Statement by Palmiro Togliatti reported in the U.S. Office of War Information, "Italian News Bulletin" (Mimeographed), May 25, 1945. In a later article, he reiterated this position. Palmiro Togliatti, *Linea d'una politica* (Milan: Milano-Sera, 1948), pp. 61–64.

2. For a comment on the Americanization of European, including Italian, sociology after World War II, see Giuseppe Galasso, "Sociologia e ricerca sociale," *Nord e Sud*, November, 1959, p. 23. On education, see Justman, *The Italian People and Their Schools*.

3. Title VI, Section I, Articles 134–37 of the Constitution of the Italian Republic.

4. For a brief discussion of American goals and interests in Italy, see the report of former Ambassador Jefferson Caffrey to the Congressional Special Committee to Study the Foreign Aid Program. *Survey No. 4 Western Europe II* (Washington, D.C.: Government Printing Office, 1957), pp. 1312–16.

5. *Ibid.*, pp. 1327–28.

6. LaPalombara, *The Italian Labor Movement*, p. 57.

7. *Ibid.*, pp. 23–29, 57, 85, 166–77.

8. Harry Goldberg, "Fiat Split Perils Free Italian Unions," *AFL-CIO Free Trade Union News*, December, 1958, p. 6.

9. See the *New York Times*, March 16, 1948, for the statement by Michael McDermott; Mrs. Luce's statements were placed in the record of the United States Senate by Senator Wayne Morse of Oregon in 1959. See the U.S. Senate, *Congressional Record—Senate*, 1959 Session, pp. 6088–89, April 27, 1959.

10. *Ibid.*

11. Toscano, "The Balance of Impotence," p. 23.

12. *La Stampa*, February 15, 1958.
13. *La Giustizia*, July 30, 1959.
14. Interview reported in *Avanti*, May 4, 1958.
15. Quoted by Tarchiani, *Dieci anni tra Roma e Washington*, p. 53.
16. *Ibid.*, p. 154.
17. *Ibid.*, pp. 139, 153, 248–49.
18. Free and Sereno, *Italy: Dependent Ally or Independent Partner?*, p. 6. These authors use the phrase "self-governing protectorate" to describe Italy vis-à-vis the United States in the early postwar years. *Ibid.*, pp. 4–7.
19. *Il Tempo*, July 15, 1958.
20. *Ibid.*, February 1, 1958.
21. However, French Socialists did not have the relationship to Communists that Italian Socialists had for a number of years after the end of World War II.
22. Free and Sereno, *Italy: Dependent Ally or Independent Partner?*, pp. 3–4.
23. Abruzzi, "Labor Supply and Productivity in Italy," p. 62.
24. Free and Sereno, *Italy: Dependent Ally or Independent Partner?*, p. 5.
25. *Ibid.*

CHAPTER 10: The Goals of Italian Foreign Policy

1. Sforza, *Cinque anni a Palazzo chigi*, p. 39.
2. Sereno, "Opinions and Attitudes of Italian Leaders," p. 30.
3. Italy, Senato della Repubblica, *Atti parlamentari*, 1st Leg., Vols. 1948–49, pp. 6534–44.
4. Statement dated December 17, 1948; Sforza, *Cinque anni a Palazzo chigi*, p. 102.
5. Martino, *L'idea liberale nella politica estera italiana*, p. 15.
6. Speech in the Chamber of Deputies, July 15, 1958. Italy, Camera dei deputati, *Atti parlamentari*, 3rd Leg., Vols. 1958, pp. 285–98.
7. *Ibid.*, October 16, 1957, 2nd Leg., Vols. 1957, pp. 33653–54.
8. Martino, *L'idea liberale nella politica estera italiana*, pp. 13–21.
9. *Il Tempo*, February 1, 1958.
10. Election speech by Martino as reported in *Il Corriere Lombardo* (Milan), April 28, 1958.
11. Martino, *L'idea liberale nella politica estera italiana*, pp. 13–21.
12. Reported in Giordano, *Il Mercato Commune e i suoi problemi*, p. 30.
13. *Il Globo*, May 6, 1958.
14. *The Italian Labor Movement*, p. 162.
15. *La Stampa*, August 4, 1958.
16. Quoted in Sforza, *Cinque anni a Palazzo chigi*, p. 221.
17. *Avanti*, May 4, 1958.
18. *Ibid.*, May 21, 1958.
19. *Ibid.*, April 29, 1958.
20. *Nord e Sud*, June, 1960, p. 6.
21. Reported in Alessandro Pizzorno, "The Italian Socialist Party and Political Participation," *PROD Translations*, December, 1959, p. 29. This statement was made at the party congress of January, 1959. Lombardi is, with Nenni, a leader of the autonomist wing of the party.
22. The text of Siri's warning is given in *Il Crociato*, March 18, 1961.

23. Pietro Nenni, "Where the Italian Socialists Stand," *Foreign Affairs*, January, 1962, p. 221.
24. *New York Times*, January 12, 1962.
25. *New York Times*, February 17, 18, 1962.
26. The quotation is taken from *Il Popolo*, July 23, 1958.
27. Statement of Foreign Minister Pella, *Relazioni Internazionali*, August 10–17, 1957, p. 993.
28. Sforza, *Cinque anni a Palazzo chigi*, pp. 266–67.
29. *New York Times*, July 22, 1959.
30. Text in Italy, Camera dei deputati, *Atti parlamentari*, 3rd Leg., Vols. 1958, pp. 93–105.
31. *Nord e Sud*, October, 1959, p. 6.
32. Gronchi, *Discorsi d'America*, pp. 50, 53.
33. Giordano, *Il Mercato Comune e i suoi problemi*, pp. 13–14.
34. Salvatorelli, *La guerra fredda*, p. 129.
35. Louis Lister, *Europe's Coal and Steel Community: An Experiment in Economic Union* (New York: Twentieth Century Fund, 1960).
36. *Il Mondo*, June 2, 1959, p. 4.
37. *Ibid.*
38. *La Stampa*, December 5, 1957.
39. *Relazioni Internazionali*, August 10–17, 1957, p. 963.
40. *Ibid.*, pp. 964–65.
41. Alessandro Fantoli, "Sulla soglia del MEC," *Nord e Sud*, July, 1959, p. 105.
42. LaPalombara, "The Utility and Limitations of Interest Group Theory in Non-American Field Situations," pp. 45–46.
43. *New York Times*, November 3, 1959.
44. *Ibid.*, December 4, 1959.
45. Abruzzi, "Labor Supply and Productivity in Italy," p. 62.
46. See report in *Il Mondo*, August 7, 1962, p. 2.
47. *Ibid.*
48. Eugenio Scalfari, "Protezione municipale, la dittatura dei doganieri," *L'Espresso*, March 23, 1958.
49. Italian Information Center, *Italian Report*, June, 1962, pp. 37–40.
50. The quotation is taken from a speech by Giuseppe Saragat, *La Giustizia*, July 6, 1958.
51. This is a summation and combination of a large number and variety of statements made by many people, official and nonofficial
52. Karl W. Deutsch and Lewis J. Edinger, *Germany Rejoins the Powers* (Stanford, Calif.: Stanford University Press, 1959), pp. 227–32.
53. "Negotiation from Strength? A Reappraisal of Western-Arab Relations," *International Affairs*, January, 1959, p. 1.
54. *La Stampa*, July 9, 1958.
55. Assemblea Costituente, *Verbale*, July 31, 1947, pp. 6543–44; also *Cinque anni a Palazzo chigi*, p. 24.
56. Assemblea Costituente, *Verbale*, July 31, 1947, p. 6553.
57. Carlo Sforza, "Italy, the Marshall Plan, and the 'Third Force,' " *Foreign Affairs*, April, 1948, p. 455.
58. Sforza, *Cinque anni a Palazzo chigi*, p. 202.
59. *Il Messagero*, June 22, 1958.

Index

INDEX

Abruzzi, Adam, 98, 114, 130
Abyssinia; *see* Ethiopia
Adenauer, Konrad, 28, 118
AFL-CIO, 101, 126, 127
Africa, interest in, 149
aggression, indirect, 135
Aglianò, Sebastiano, 5
agricultural organizations, 102–4
Agriculture, Ministry of, 104
aid, economic, 126, 127
air bases, American, 126
Alessandrini, Adolfo, 118
Algeria, 24
Anfuso, Filippo, 54
anticlericalism, 124
antitrust legislation, 91–92
Antonini, Luigi, 126
armed forces, *see* military
Atlanticists, 8, 136
atomic neutralization, 140
Austria-Hungary, 33
autarchy, 30, 34
Axis, Rome-Berlin, 108

Badini Confalonieri, Vittorio, 66
Badoglio, Pietro, 34
balance of power, 39–40
Banfield, Edward C., 4, 7
banking, 88
Bernabei, Ettore, 118
big business, 87–97
 and the Church, 78
 political failure of, 34
 and ruling class, 11
bishops, influence of, 78
 see also Roman Catholic Church
Bissolati, Leonida, 37

Boldrini, Marcello, 88, 96
Bologna Center, Johns Hopkins University, 112
Bonomi, Paolo, 103–4
Borgese, Giuseppe, 7, 15, 29
Brosio, Manlio, 117
bureaucracy
 and big business, 91
 and intellectuals, 105
 and the ruling class, 11

Cabinet, 67–71
Calabria, 5
Carducci, Giosuè, 7
Carristi, 58, 140
Casardi, Alberico, 117
Catholic Action Society, 51, 77, 140–41
 see also Roman Catholic Church
Catholic Church; *see* Roman Catholic Church
Catholic University of the Sacred Heart, 42
Cavour, Camillo Benso di, 31, 37, 42, 56
CGIL (Italian General Confederation of Labor), 63, 98–102, 126
Chamber of Deputies, 48–49, 65–67
checks and balances, 14
China, Communist, 94
Christian Democratic Party (DC), 14, 20–21, 47, 96, 115, 116, 131, 144
 and agriculture, 103–4
 and ENI, 97
 internal organization of, 49–52
 and "opening to the left," 141–42
 and Roman Catholic Church, 77–78

178 *Index*